영어로 말하는 영어수업

조인숙 지음

한국문화사

영어로 말하는 영어수업

초판인쇄 2011년 10월 25일
초판발행 2011년 10월 31일

지 은 이 조 인 숙
꾸 민 이 이 지 은
펴 낸 이 김 진 수
펴 낸 곳 **한국문화사**
등   록 1991년 11월 9일 제2-1276호
주   소 서울특별시 성동구 아차산로 3(성수동 1가) 502호
전   화 (02)464-7708 / 3409-4488
전   송 (02)499-0846
이 메 일 hkm7708@hanmail.net
홈페이지 www.hankookmunhwasa.co.kr

ISBN 978-89-5726-913-8 93700

머리말

1997년 초등교육과정에 영어 교과가 도입된 이후 현재의 초등영어교육은 '활동' 위주의 수업이 되었다 해도 과언이 아니다. 이는 그동안 중·고등학교에서의 영어교육이 학습자의 흥미와 관심을 고려하지 않고 기계적이고 피상적인 학습에 그쳤던 것에 대한 반발과 무관하지 않다. 어린이 영어 수업에서의 '활동'은 어린이들의 특성을 고려하고 그들의 관심과 흥미를 이끌어내어 학습의 효과를 증진시키기 위해 고안된 것이다.

사실 초창기에는 주입식 문법 교육과 맥락에서 고립된 어휘의 축적에 익숙한 대부분의 영어 교사들이 학생들 앞에서 노래하고 율동을 선보이고 게임을 진행한다는 것이 어색하고 부자연스러웠다. 특히 스토리텔링의 장점과 가치가 부각되면서 영어 수업 시간의 유익한 활동 하나를 위해 스토리 암기는 물론 캐릭터의 목소리와 표정, 그리고 몸동작까지 구사하고 이해를 돕기 위한 그림 자료 등을 준비해야 하니 교사의 부담은 더욱 가중될 수밖에 없었다.

그럼에도 불구하고 영어 수업에서 노래, 챈트, 율동, 게임, 스토리텔링, 연극, 뮤지컬, 마술, 요리, 종이접기 및 만들기 등과 같은 다양한 '활동'은 빠뜨릴 수 없는 요소가 되었고 교사들은 이러한 '활동'을 원어민 교사의 자연스러운 영어 구사에 대체하였다. 즉 TEE (Teaching English in English-영어로 진행하는 영어수업)가 힘겨운 교사들은 많은 활동과 자료를 준비하여 학생들을 그러한 활동에 참여시키는 것으로 수업을 진행하는 것에 만족하였다.

그런데 이런 활동 위주의 수업은 일시적인 흥미와 관심을 제공할 뿐 그 이상의 발전을 가져오지 못했다. 학생들은 수업을 통해 다른 교과나 일상생활에 연계할 수 있는 주요 아이디어에 대한 이해 없이 단편적인 사실의 암기와 주제와 관련 없는 활동에 참여하였고 교사는 TEE를 가능케 하는 자신의 영어 숙련도를 향상시키기 위해 수업 준비 이외의 시간과 노력을 투자해야 했다.

*영어로 말하는 영어수업(TEE for Understanding)*은 틀에 박힌 활동 위주의 수업에서 벗어나 실생활과 관련된 구체적인 목표를 설정하고 그 결과를 이끌어내기 위해 활동을 사용하는 수업, 또한 교사와 학생들의 사고를 자극하여 더 나은 방향으로 수업을 발전시키는 계기

를 마련하고자 집필되었다. 이 책에는 15개의 토픽에 대한 수업지도안과 4개의 전래동화가 수록되어 있다. 각각의 토픽은 부제를 가지고 있으며 목표(Goals), 발문(Questions), 과업(Tasks), 교수보조물(Teaching Aids), 주의사항(Note), 수업의 요지(Gist of a Lesson)가 세부 수업지도안(Teaching and Learning Plan) 앞에 명시되어 있다. 또한 세부 수업지도안 뒤의 'To Better Teachers'에서는 수업과 관련된 정보를 좀 더 제공한다.

목표(Goals)는 그 수업을 통해 학생들이 이해하기를 바라는 것—아는 것에서 그치는 것이 아니라 활용하고 공감할 수 있는 것—이며 기존의 활동중심 수업에서 쉽게 볼 수 있는 예상가능하고 판에 박힌 목표에서 벗어나고자 하였다. 발문(Questions)은 설정된 목표를 달성하기 위해 그 수업의 주요 아이디어(Main Idea)를 묻는 것으로 단편적인 사실이 아닌 전이 가능한 사고를 요한다. 수업지도안(Teaching and Learning Plan)에서의 발문은 " "안에 진한 글씨체로 표시되어 있다. 과업(Tasks)은 발문과 동일선상에서 학생들이 수행해야 하는 것이며 이를 통해 설정된 목표의 성취여부를 확인할 수 있다. 여기에서는 개인별 수행 과제보다 그룹별 수행과제의 비중이 더 크다. 교수보조물(Teaching Aids)은 교실에 비치되어 있는 시청각 기자재는 제외하고 그 수업에 필요한 준비물을 보여준다. 주의사항(Note)은 주의할 점이나 기억해야 할 사항이고 수업의 요지(Gist of the Lesson)는 수업의 요약본이라 할 수 있는데 발문과 활동 위주로 수업의 흐름을 파악할 수 있도록 하였다.

하나의 토픽은 한 시간 분량이 아니며 교사는 학습자의 연령과 수준별로 1~3주에 거쳐 본 교재를 토대로 세부계획안을 만들어 활용할 수 있다. Topic 4, Topic 8, Topic 12, 그리고 Topic 15 뒤에는 전래 동화가 수록되어 있다. 전래 동화는 8장면으로 구성되어 있으며 각 장면 하단에 <My story> 공간이 있다. 이 공란은 다음과 같이 각 장면을 요약하거나 주요 표현을 골라 챈트를 만들거나 혹은 퀴즈를 내는 용도로 활용할 수 있다. 스토리 앞부분에 있는 공란에는 해당 이야기에 대한 목표, 발문, 과업, 교수보조물, 주의사항 및 수업의 요지를 기록해보도록 한다.

Mr. Moon and Miss Sun Scene 1	The Lazy Man Scene 2	The Snail Lady Scene 3
Chant 1 ♪ A long time ago, there lived a tiger. ♪ A long time ago, there lived a fox. ♪ A long time ago, there lived a cat. ♪ A long time ago, there lived a bird.	Remember 1. Why are you making an ox? 2. Can I try it on?	Scene 3 ●She cleaned the house, washed his clothes and mended some of his old clothing. ●Would you be my wife?

영어로 말하는 영어수업에서는 교사의 몸짓, 손동작, 얼굴표정, 실물, 그림, Video 등의 활용이 필수적이다. 수업지도안에서 교사는 T로 학생 한 명과 학생 여러 명은 몇몇 경우를 제외하고는 구별 없이 S로 표기하였다. 학생들은 교사의 발문에 짝이나 그룹원들과 함께 의논하고 상의하며 수다나 잡담이 아닌 과제 수행 시간으로 영어로 이야기할 수 있도록 노력해야 한다.

교사는 학생들의 그룹을 돌면서 우리말을 영어로 바꾸어 주고 아이디어를 제시해 주어야 하기 때문에 그 수업의 발문에서 나올 수 있는 예상 답변을 미리 준비하고 있어야 한다. 교사는 동시통역에 대한 부담을 갖지 말고 처음에는 주요 단어만 그 다음에는 점차적으로 구와 문장으로 확대시키도록 한다.

이 책이 제시하는 수업의 핵심은 교사가 '활동'을 고민하는 것이 아니라 '전이 가능한 아이디어'는 무엇이며 '어떤 결과'에 도달해야 하는지(어떤 목표를 성취해야 하는지) 그 결과에 도달하기 위해서는 '어떤 질문'을 던져야 하고 목표를 성취했음을 보여줄 '과업(수행과제)'은 무엇인지를 고민하는 것이다. 발문에 대한 '예상 답변'을 고민하고 기록하다보면 교사의 사고력과 숙련도(proficiency)까지도 동시에 향상될 것이다.

끝으로 *영어로 말하는 영어수업(TEE for Understanding)*이 나올 수 있도록 많은 격려와 조언을 해주신 선생님들과 실제 수업 현장에서 아이디어를 제공해준 어린이 친구들, 그리고 여러 면에서 애를 써주신 한국문화사 관계자 여러분께 깊은 감사의 말씀을 전한다.

2011년 9월
조 인 숙

■ 차례

Greetings
Nice to meet you!

Goals	• **Students can introduce themselves.** • **Students can understand rules to obey in the classroom.**
Questions	• Why do you say hi when you meet someone? • What do you want to say about yourself? • Are rules in the classroom important? • What are 'dos an don'ts' in the classroom?
Task	• Students exchange greetings and introduce themselves. • Students can make nickname tags. • Students talk about rules in the classroom. • Students complete a list of 'dos and don'ts' in the classroom.
Teaching Aids	dolls(rabbit and turtle), nickname tags, paper

Note

수업을 처음 시작할 때 자기소개 시간을 갖게 되는데 인사는 왜 필요한지, 스스로에 대해 소개할 때는 어떤 것을 이야기하고 싶은지, 또한 앞으로 수업에서 지켜야 할 예의나 규칙은 무엇인지 교사가 지정해주는 것이 아니라 학생들이 서로 상의하여 결론을 내릴 수 있는 분위기를 만들어 준다.

Gist of a Lesson

Starting a Lesson		
▪ Greeting ▪ Warm-Up	▪ 교사 본인 소개, 그룹 만들기	● 이름 쪽지
Developing a Lesson		
▪ Activity 1	▪ 토끼와 거북의 막대 인형을 준비해서 역할극을 보여준다. (인사 및 간단히 자기소개 하는 방법 보여주기)	● 막대 인형
▪ Essential Question 1	▪ Why do you say hi when you meet someone? (누군가를 만나면 왜 인사하는 걸까요?)	● 개별 답변
▪ Essential Question 2	▪ What do you want to say about yourself? (자기소개 할 때 어떤 것을 말하고 싶어요?)	● 그룹 활동
▪ Activity 2	▪ 토끼와 거북의 대화 듣고 애칭 이해하기 (각자의 이름표 만들기)	● 카드 종이
▪ Essential Question 3	▪ Are rules in the classroom important? (학급에서의 규칙은 중요한가요?)	● 개별 답변
▪ Essential Question 4	▪ What are 'dos an don'ts' in the classroom? (학급에서는 어떤 규칙을 지켜야 할까요?)	● 그룹 활동
▪ Activity 3	▪ 학급의 규칙 목록 작성하기	● 종이
Ending a Lesson		
▪ Wrap-Up	▪ 배운 내용 요약	

Teaching and Learning Plan

Starting a Lesson

T: Hello, everyone.

S: Hello.

T: How are you today?

I am Veronica. You can call me Veronica or just Teacher.

I am so happy to see you all.

I hope we have a great time for a year.

(교사는 다음과 같이 자기소개를 할 수도 있다.)

T: Hello.

My name is Veronica.

Nice to meet you all.

I like reading books and listening to music.

I hope we have a great time together.

(교사는 학생들의 어색한 분위기를 깨기 위해서 그룹을 만들 수 있다. 과일이나 꽃 혹은 동물이나 사물의 이름이 적힌 쪽지를 고르도록 해서 같은 이름을 가진 학생들끼리 그룹을 형성해 모여 앉도록 한다.)

➤첫 수업은 다소 어색한 분위기에서 이루어지므로 교사는 활기찬 수업이 될 수 있도록 많은 준비를 해야 한다.

Developing a Lesson

T: (R)Hello. Hello.

What's this sound? (동작을 취한다.)

There must be someone around here. Who are you? Can you tell us about you? (손 인형이나 막대인형을 꺼내며) (R)Hi, I'm Rabbit. Nice to meet you. I'm from the woods.

I like running. (T)Me. Me. I want to meet new friends, too. There

➤(R)은 토끼이고 (T)는 거북이므로 그에 맞게 목소리를 바꾼다. 교사가 학생들에게 토끼와 거북을 소개시키는 1인 3역 역할극이다.
가르치는 대상의 연령이나 취향에 맞는 캐릭터나 연예인 등을 등장인물로 활용할 수 있다.

9

is another friend. Do you want to meet him?

S: Yes.

T: (T)Hello. My name is Turtle. I am 10 years old. I like swimming in the sea. Nice to meet you all.

S: Nice to meet you.

T: What do you say when you meet someone?(응답)
"Why do you say hi when you meet someone?"
우리는 누군가를 만나면 왜 인사할까요?

S: 응답한다.

T: (교사는 학생들의 응답을 영어로 바꾸어 다시 이야기 한다.) We want to be good people. Good people have good manners. That's why we should say hello/hi with big smiles. Right?

T: Do you want to have good manners? Why don't you look at each other and say hi/hello?

S: 학생들은 서로 마주보고 인사한다.

T: Good.

T: When you introduce yourself, what would you like to say about yourself? Do you want to talk about family? For example, I have two brothers, one sister and parents in my family. Or do you want to talk about your hobbies? I play computer games in my free time. I love watching TV everyday. (동작과 함께 몇 가지 예를 들어준다.)

T: "What do you want to say about yourself?" 여러분은 자기소개를 할 때 어떤 것을 이야기하고 싶어요?

S: Hobby, Dream, Family……. (응답한다.)

T: You want to talk about your hobbies and dreams. I see. Now shall we practice together?

S: 학생들은 그룹원과 함께 서로서로 인사하고 자신을 소개한다.

T: 교사는 그룹을 돌며 우리말을 영어로 바꾸어준다.

➜교사의 질문을 학생들이 이해하지 못했을 경우 한국어로 이야기하고 다시 한 번 영어로 반복한다. 학생들은 한국어로 답변할 수 있으며 교사가 주요 내용을 영어로 바꾸어주면 기억하여 다시 한 번 이야기할 수 있도록 한다.

➜가장 좋은 설명은 풍부한 예문이다. 평소에 좋은 예문을 메모해두는 습관을 기르도록 한다.

➜교사는 질문에 가능한 답변을 영어로 표현할 수 있도록 준비해 둔다.

- I like <u>teaching</u>. I want to be <u>a teacher</u>.
- My hobby is <u>playing games</u>.
  I like <u>playing games</u>.
- words about task: teaching, curing, helping people, rescuing / saving, reporting, fixing, helping animals, selling, making, taking pictures, practicing law, growing flowers, flying an airplane, etc.
- words about jobs: a teacher, a doctor, a police officer, a fire fighter, a reporter, a mechanic, a vet, a salesclerk, a factory worker, a photographer, a lawyer, a florist, a pilot, etc.
- words about hobbies: playing games, reading books, listening to music, watching TV, drawing/painting, singing, dancing, searching the Internet, exercising, playing the piano/violin/flute/cello, going to see a movie, etc.

T: Okay, now listen to Rabbit and Turtle. (두 인형이 마주보고 대화하는 장면을 연출한다.)

(R) Hi, I'm Rabbit.

(T) Hi, I'm Turtle.

(R) Nice to meet you, Turtle.

(T) Nice to meet you, Rabbit.

(R) I'm from the woods. Where are you from?

(T) I'm from the sea.

(R) I like running. Do you like running?

(T) No. I like swimming. I want to be a swimmer.

(R) Really? I want to be a runner.

(T) I see. By the way, do you have a nickname? I am Tom.

(R) I am Ron.

(T) Nice meeting you, Ron. See you later.

(R) Bye Tom.

T: Do you remember Rabbit's nickname?

S: Ron.

T: Good. Here is a name tag. His nickname is Ron. Let's put it here

(이름표를 토끼 인형에 붙여준다). And what's Turtle's nickname?

S: Tom.

T: Right. His nickname is Tom. Here we go(거북 이름표를 학생들에게 보여주고 인형에 붙인다).

T: Well, can you think of your own nicknames? Let's make our nickname tags like Ron Rabbit and Tom Turtle. Get one of these sheets of paper and pass them around. If you need some help, just call Teacher. I'm ready to help you, okay?

S: 영어 시간에 사용할 자신의 애칭을 생각해서 이름표를 만든다.

T: Well done. Everyone has a beautiful name tag. Can you introduce yourselves now? Excellent. Who can start first?

S: Me.

T: Wow, we have a brave volunteer. Would you come up to the front and introduce yourself to the classmates?

S: 이름표를 단 학생들이 한 명씩 앞으로 나와 본인 소개를 한다.

T: 자발적인 분위기가 형성되지 않으면 자기소개를 한 학생이 다른 학생을 지목할 수 있도록 한다. 자기소개가 아닌 친구소개를 하는 시간을 만들어도 좋다.

(교사는 다음과 같은 활동을 할 수 있다.)

T: Thank you, everyone. Let's see we can chant together. You tell your name and ask 'who are you?' The next person says his/her name and asks 'who are you?' You've got it? Let me start first (손뼉을 치거나 동작을 취하며 한사람씩 돌아간다). I am Veronica. Who are you? I am John. Who are you? I am Mary. Who are you? (처음에는 천천히 하고 점점 빠른 박자에 맞추어 본다.)

► chant ◄

I am (name). Who are you?

────

→교사가 학생 수에 맞도록 영어 이름을 준비해서 학생들이 마음에 드는 것을 고르도록 한다. 이름을 조사할 때에는 의미도 함께 기록해서 학생들에게 제공한다.

→ 자기소개 방식
Introduction
-Greeting
Body
-Name
-Hometown
-School/Work
-Free Time/Hobby
-Hopes/Dreams
Conclusion
-Closing

T: Wonderful. Now it is a little more difficult. I'll start first. I am Veronica. I like dancing. I'll be a dancer. It is challenging, isn't it? Let's try together. I am John. I like books. I'll be a writer. Very good. One more try. I am Mary. I like flowers. I'll be a florist....... (이와 같은 방식으로 박자를 맞추어 본인을 소개해 본다.)

► chant ◄

I am (name).

I like (things or doing).

I'll be a (job).

T: Thank you everyone. Danny, who do you think is a good teacher?

S: A wise and humorous teacher.

T: Danny thinks a good teacher is a wise and humorous one. How about you, Gina? Who is a good teacher?

S: 쉽게 설명해주시는 선생님이요.

T: A person who explains something clearly and easily.

Then how about a good student? Who is a good student?

S: A student who listens to the teacher.

A student who doesn't make any noise.

A students who never tells a lie.

T: I see. Thank you, everyone.

Let's try to be ideal teacher and students together, okay?

T: Do you think there should be some rules in the classroom?

S: Yes, I do.

T: "Are rules in the classroom important?" 학급에서의 규칙은 중요한가요? Why do you think so?

S: A classroom is not a private area.

We should consider others and try to make good environment.

T: Right. Students come to school to learn not only knowledge but

➤교사는 이상적인 교사의 모습으로 학생들이 이야기하는 것을 판서한다.

➤교사는 학생들이 이상적인 학생의 모습으로 기술하는 것을 요약하여 판서 한다.

13

also manners. Thank you for your answer.

T: Then "What are 'dos and don'ts' in the classroom?" 학급에서 지켜야할 규칙에는 어떤 것이 있을까요? What we should or should not do during the class? Talk about them with your group members and write them down on the paper (교사는 교실에서의 규칙 목록을 적을 수 있는 종이를 나누어 주고 각 그룹을 돌며 학생들의 의견을 듣는다).

T: Have you finished? Let me see. Would you put yours on the board?
S: 목록을 게시한다.
T: Thank you. We should help, share, clean up and wait for the turn.
We should not yell, fight, tell a lie and say bad words. Good job. Now let's choose the most important rules.
S: 자신들이 작성한 규칙 목록 중에서 겹쳐지거나 가장 중요하다고 생각되는 공통의 규칙을 선정한다.
T: (교사는 학생들이 선정한 규칙을 깨끗한 종이에 옮겨 적는다.)
This is our 'dos and don'ts' in the classroom. Can you keep the rules?
S: Yes.
T: Excellent.

(활용 어휘)

- words about rules: Do your homework, Listen to the teacher, Share with friends, Be nice to friends, Wait your turn, Do not yell, Do not fight, Do not say bad words, Do not pick on friends, Do not tell a lie, etc.

T: Today we talked about people with good manners exchange greetings starting with 'Hello or Hi'.

S: Hello. Hi.

T: Also we learned how to introduce ourselves like "Hello, I am Veronica. Nice to meet you. I like dancing. I want to be a dancer." Can all of you introduce yourselves at the same time?

S: 학생들은 다함께 동시에 본인소개를 한다.

T: Wow. Hope you have good manners and feel confident when you introduce yourselves.

S: Okay.

T: You said rules in the classroom are important. We chose our rules in the classroom. Look at this. Let's read them together.

S: 규칙을 함께 읽는다.

T: Actions are louder than words. You should keep them.

T: Stand up everyone and make a line please. Line up.
Give me five one by one! See you next time.

S: Bye.

To Better Teachers

성공적인 영어 학습을 위해서 지켜야 할 약속이 있다. 그것을 4Ps라 정하자.

첫 번째 P는 Purpose(목적)이다. 영어 학습을 위해서는 목적이나 목표가 있어야 한다. 목표가 구체적일수록 달성하기가 용이하다. 나의 목표는 무엇인지 생각해 보자.

두 번째 P는 Passion(열정)이다. 관심과 애정을 가지고 배우고 익히는 것에 열중해야 효과적인 영어 학습을 할 수 있다.

세 번째 P는 불안감이나 지루함을 견뎌내는 Patience(인내심 혹은 끈기)이다. 목적을 달성하기 위해서는 끝까지 참고 중도 포기의 유혹을 이겨내야 할 것이다. 영어 학습이 항상 즐거운 것만은 아니다.

마지막의 P는 Practice(연습)이다. Practice makes Perfect(연습은 완벽을 만든다)라는 말이 있다. 하루 2시간씩 혹은 그 이상씩 꾸준히 연습해 보자. 6개월이 지나면 달라진 모습을 발견할 수 있을 것이다.

이렇게 4Ps를 마음속에 새기고 실천할 것을 약속하며 연습할 표현을 살펴보자.

⊃ Answer the following questions.

1. Do you like jazz?

2. Are you interested in movies?

3. Do you have much money to spend?

4. Do you exercise everyday?

5. Do you get along well with your family?

⊃ Now Answer again using following expressions.

1. Do you like jazz?

   Yes. I like jazz and Ryan does, too.

2. Are you interested in movies?

   No. I am not interested in movies and Tom isn't, either.

3. Do you have much money to spend?

   No. I don't have much money to spend, but Bill does.

4. Do you exercise everyday?

   Yes. I do exercise everyday, but not my husband.

5. Do you get along well with your family?

   Yes. I get along really well with my family but Harry doesn't.

⊃ What three things would you like to change in your life?

Compare your answers with the following examples.

1. I was not interested in movies, but I'll go to see a movie often to improve English skills.

2. I didn't exercise at all, but I'll work out regularly to keep in shape.

3. I didn't get along with my family, but I'll try to be nice to my family from now on.

이번에는 'Dos and Don'ts'에 대해 좀 더 살펴보자. 해야 할 일 혹은 할 수 있는 일은 'Do'에 '-s'를 붙인 'Dos'라고 하고, 하지 말아야 할 일 혹은 할 수 없는 일은 'Don't'에 '-s'를 붙여서 'Don'ts'라고 한다. 우리가 일상생활에서 경험하는 'Dos'와 'Don'ts'는 상황에 따라 다양하므로 개별적으로 필요한 것은 따로 기록해 두고 여기에서는 영어권 국가 중에 영어의 발생지인 영국에 갔을 때 알아두면 좋을 'Dos and Don'ts'를 먼저 살펴보고, 외국인이 우리나라에서 생활할 때 조언할 수 있는 'Dos and Don'ts'와 비교해 보자.

〈영국에서의 'Dos and Don'ts'〉

Dos	Don'ts
1. Do stand in line.	1. Do not greet people with a kiss.
2. Do say "Excuse Me."	2. Do not make gestures such as back-slapping and hugging.
3. Do say "Please" and "Thank you."	3. Do not talk loudly in public.
4. Do say sorry.	4. Do not stare at anyone in public.
5. Do shake hands.	5. Do not spit.
6. Do smile.	6. Do not ask personal questions including asking a lady her age.
7. Do cover your mouth when yawning or coughing.	7. Do not eat off a knife when having a meal.
8. Do open doors for other people.	8. Do not speak with your mouth full of food.
9. Do drive on the left side of the road.	9. Do not burp in public.
10. Do take your hat off when you go indoors(men only).	10. Do not pick your nose in public.

〈한국에서의 Dos and Don'ts〉

1. Do not show anger and criticism.

Showing anger is impolite and can damage interpersonal relationship. Keep your temper at all times. Also avoid criticism whenever possible. When absolutely necessary, it must be done tactfully, gently and privately.

2. Do not bargain at supermarkets or department stores.

In markets, we are expected to bargain. After asking the price, we give the seller a counter-offer. Finally we agree on a price somewhere between the seller's offer and our own. But we should not bargain at supermarkets, department stores, or other places where the price is already marked.

3. Do show kindness and respect to elderly people.

When we greet elderly people, we bow. We offer bus or subway seats to them. When they have trouble crossing the street, or trouble carrying something, we help them. Also we use two hands when passing objects.

4. Do prepare gifts when visiting someone's home.

When visiting someone's home, we take gifts such as fruit, flowers, cakes, or alcohol. On special occasions, such as a first birthday, a wedding, a 60th birthday party or a funeral, we put some money in an envelop as a gift.

5. Do not talk too much during the meal.

We use chopsticks and a large spoon when eating the meal. Rice is served on the left and soup on the right. The senior or the superior person usually begins the meal. But we should not talk too much during the meal. Also rice is the staple of the Korean diet. Throwing away leftover rice is considered wasteful and bad luck.

6. Do not call Koreans by their given names.

We usually address each other as Mr. Kim, Miss Yang, or by the titles like Manager Kim, Chairman Lee, or by the occupation such as Driver Park or Electrician Song. So it is advisable not to stress familiarity calling given names until the appropriate time. Mothers are often referred to as their child's mother, for example Seo-young's Mother.

7. Do not worry about personal questions.

Personal questions are a way of getting to know another person. You don't have to answer the private questions correctly. If you do not wish to answer them, simply change the subject. These questions may include 'Why aren't you married?', 'How old are you?', 'Where are you going?', 'What are you doing?' and so on.

⟨Your 'Dos and Dont's'⟩

Dos	Don'ts

Classroom Objects & Actions
What's this in English?

Goals	**Students can identify classroom objects and actions.**
Questions	• Do you think Konglish expressions English? • What is your ideal classroom? What do you need in the classroom?
Task	• Students describe the classroom where they are and their ideal classrooms. • Students find Konglish expressions and correct them. • Students give and follow simple classroom commands.
Teaching Aids	mask, baton, classroom picture/photo, Konglish words

Note

흔히 학급에서 볼 수 있는 사물은 'What's this?'라는 질문에 'It's a____'로 기계적인 답변을 암기시키는 경우가 많다. 우리가 사용하는 단어 중에 Konglish 표현을 알아보고 학생들이 생각하는 이상적인 교실을 기술하기 위해서는 사물의 이름을 인지해야 함을 이해시킨다. 학급에서의 활동 어휘는 TPR(Total Physical Response)을 통해 습득할 수 있도록 한다.

Gist of a Lesson

Starting a Lesson		
▪ Greeting ▪ Routine Questions ▪ Checking Attendance ▪ Warm-Up	▪ 캐나다 친구인 Bill 소개하기	● 가면
Developing a Lesson		
▪ Activity 1	▪ Bill의 우리말 배우기 (교실에 있는 사물의 한국어와 영어 이름을 비교해 본다.)	● 지시봉
▪ Essential Question 1	▪ Do you think Konglish expressions English? (콩글리시는 영어인가요?)	● 개별 답변
▪ Activity 2	▪ Bill의 교실과 실제 교실 비교해 보기 (그림/사진 속 교실과 실제교실의 공통점과 차이점 찾기)	● 교실 그림 /사진
▪ Essential Question 2	▪ What is your ideal classroom? What do you need in the classroom?	● 그룹 활동
▪ Activity 3	▪ 이상적인 교실 그리기 (어떤 물건이 왜 필요한지 생각하면서 그림을 그린 다.)	● 그림 종이
▪ Activity 4 ▪ Activity 5	▪ 콩글리시 표현을 올바른 영어 표현으로 바꿔보기 ▪ 교사의 지시 듣고 동작 취하기(TPR)	● 단어 카드
Ending a Lesson		
▪ Wrap-Up	▪ 배운 내용 요약	

Teaching and Learning Plan

Starting a Lesson

T: Hello, everyone.

How are you doing?

S: Good.

T: Pretty good? That's good!

Look outside. How's the weather today? Is it rainy?

S: No.

T: Is it sunny outside?

S: Yes.

T: I love a warm and bright day like today.

Stand up(동작과 함께). Look at each other and exchange greetings.

S: 학생들은 서로 인사를 나눈다.

T: Good. Sit down.

S: 자리에 앉는다.

T: Close your eyes.

S: 눈을 감는다.

Let me introduce someone special. Close your eyes, please.

Do not open your eyes, yet. (교사는 (머리에) 가면을 쓴다.)

Now open your eyes.

S: 눈을 뜬다.

T: Hi, everyone. My name is Bill.

I'm from Canada. Nice to meet you.

I am learning Korean nowadays. Korean is very beautiful.

Actually I have lots of things to ask.

Can you answer my questions?

S: Yes.

T: Thank you.

→학생들에게 지시할 때에는 동작을 함께 보여준다. 교사의 지시에 학생들은 구두로 반응할 필요는 없으며 행동으로 옮기면 된다.

→학생들이 좋아하는 캐릭터나 연예인 가면을 준비해도 좋다. 종이로 띠를 만들어 앞부분에 사진을 풀로 붙이거나 펠트에 고무줄을 연결한 띠를 만들어 두면 다양한 캐릭터를 붙여 사용할 수 있다. 코팅한 캐릭터의 뒷면에 벨크로 테이프를 붙여둔다.

T: What's this in Korean?((손가락) 지시봉으로 연필을 가리킨다.)

S: 연필.

T: I see. A pencil. We say a pencil. What about this one? (책가방을 가리키며) How do you say it in Korean?

S: 가방.

T: A backpack. We say a backpack in English.
Oh, (압정을 가리키며) this is a thumbtack. We call it a thumbtack. What's this in Korean?

S: 압정.

T: Thank you.

T: (스프링노트를 잡고) I have this in my country. How do you say this in Korean? What's this in Korean?

S: 스프링노트.

T: Do you mean a springnote? Is it Korean?

S: Yes.

T: Yes? It sounds English, but it is not. It must be Konglish. Konglish is Korean-style English. **"Do you think Konglish expressions are English?"** 콩글리시가 영어인가요?

S: No, they are not English. (학생들은 콩글리시가 왜 영어가 아닌지 이유를 설명한다.)

T: Konglish expressions are not English because only Koreans understand them. Language is used to communicate. When we converse with someone in English, we should use correct expressions that he or she can understand.
We'd better change Konglish expressions into correct English expressions. Instead of a springnote, we can say a spiral notebook.

S: A spiral notebook.

T: (리모컨을 집어 들고) How do you say this in Korean?

➤ 'Konglish'자체는 영어지만 콩글리시 표현은 영어가 아니다. 'Spanglish'는 스페인식 영어라는 영어 단어이고 그 표현은 영어가 아니다. 'Japlish'는 일본식 영어란 의미의 영단어이고 그 표현은 영어가 아니다.

S: 리모컨.

T: A remocon is Konglish. We say a remote control. Is it too long? You can make it short like a 'remote'. So 리모컨 is a remote control or a remote in English.

S: A remote control. A remote.

T: (에어컨을 가리키며) What's this in Korean? How do you say it in Korean?

S: 에어컨.

T: An aircon? I'm sorry. This is not English. It's Konglish. In English, it is an air conditioner.

S: An air conditioner.

T: We say an air conditioner.

S: An air conditioner.

T: I brought a picture of my classroom in Canada.

T: Look around your classroom and look at the picture. I hope you find the difference between yours and mine. Thank you for your kindness. See you again. Bye(마스크를 벗는다).

T: Wow. Bill is a good student and a good teacher, too. Look at this picture. It is Bill's classroom. Look at the picture carefully and find the difference between our classroom and his classroom.

→Bill이 발견한 Konglish 표현을 바르게 바꾸면:
❶ a springnote
 -a spiral notebook
❷ a remocon
 - a remote control
❸ an aircon
 - an air conditioner

→교실 그림은 그림 사전이나 학교를 배경으로 하는 영화 속에서 찾아본다. 좌측의 사진과 그림은 참고용이므로 수업 내용과 일치하지 않는다.

Bill has a globe in his classroom. We don't have it. We have a map though. Can you talk about it in a group?

S: 학생들은 자신들의 교실과 Bill의 교실을 비교해 본다.

➤교사가 준비한 사진/그림 속의 교실과 실제 교실을 비교해서 공통점과 차이점을 이야기해 본다.

T: Did you find the difference? What is it?

S: A pencil sharpener. Bill has a big pencil sharpner.

T: We have it, too. Here we go. We have the pencil sharpener, though it is very small.

S: A vase with flowers.

T: That's right. We don't have a vase with flowers but we have several plant pots.

S: Who are they? This person is a teacher and this person is a teacher's aide. She is helping the teacher and the students.

T: Well, let's think about the ideal classroom. **"What is your ideal classroom? What do you need in the classroom?"** 여러분이 꿈꾸는 이상적인 교실은 어떤 곳일까요? 어떤 물건이 있을까요?

➤학생들은 자신들이 생각하는 이상적인 교실에 대해 그룹원들과 이야기를 나눈다.

S: 학생들은 각자가 생각하는 이상적인 교실에 어떤 물건이 있는지 그룹원들과 이야기를 나눈다.

T: 교사는 그룹을 돌면서 학생들이 영어로 이야기 할 수 있도록 돕는다.

활용 구문 및 어휘

- My ideal classroom has _____.
  There is/are _____ in my ideal classroom.
- words about classroom objects: a chalk board, a white board, a computer, a television, a DVD player, a stereo/CD player, a map, a screen, a P.A.(public address) system, a clock, teacher's desk, a bulletin board, a globe, a waste basket, a bookcase/bookshelf, etc.

➤학생들이 그림을 설명을 할 때는 활용 구문을 제시하여 단어만 바꿔 쓸 수 있도록 한다.

T: Take one and pass out the sheets of paper. Draw your ideal classroom. I hope you think about the reason why you need such classroom objects.

S: 이상적인 교실에는 어떤 물건이 필요한지 생각하면서 그림을 그린다.

T: Are you finished? Now show us your picture and describe it, please. Danny, would you show your picture?

S: 그림을 기술한다.

T: You have a big hanger. It's a good idea. We can hang our heavy coats on the hanger instead of chairs or floor. Thank you Danny. Jina, how about you?

S: 그림을 설명한다.

T: You have a dictionary. During the break, you can look up some words you don't know well. Very good. You are a devoted student. Thanks. Sue, you have a bed. Why do we need a bed in the classroom?

S: 침대가 왜 교실에 있는지 설명한다.

T: You are thoughtful. Disabled students can study with us. That's a great idea. (학생들의 그림설명이 끝나고 나서) I was so impressed with your great ideas. Well done, everyone.

T: Stand up quietly. Make a line, please. Come to the front desk and pick one piece of paper. On the piece of paper, there is a Konglish word. Think about the correct English word.

S: 학생들이 콩글리시 표현을 올바른 영어표현으로 바꿔 보도록 한다.

➡실생활에서 우리가 사용하는 콩글리시 표현을 찾아오도록 해서 정보를 공유하는 시간을 만들어본다.

T: Zoe, what is your word?

S: 핸드폰.

T: A handphone is correct?

S: No. A moving phone.

T: A moving phone, you said? Hmm, good try, but not quite right. It is a cellular or cell phone. A handphone is Konglish and a cell phone is English.

- words about Konglish expressions: 샤프(펜)(a mechanical pencil), 커닝
(cheating), 에어컨(an air conditioner), 리모컨(a remote control), 스프링노트(a
spiral notebook), 핸드폰(a cellular phone/a mobile phone), 카레라이스(curry
and rice), 아파트(an apartment(house/building)), 슈퍼(a supermarket), 라벨(a
label), (자동차)핸들(a steering wheel), 사이다(sprite, seven-up), etc.

T: During the class, I gave you some classroom commands like
'Stand up'. Can you tell me what you remember?

S: Close your eyes.

T: Good. (동작과 함께) 'Look at the picture', 'Sit down', 'Make
a line', etc. What else do most teachers usually say?

S: Be quiet.

T: Would you make gestures with me? (동작과 함께) Be quiet,
Answer the questions, Say it, Read it, Write it, Listen carefully.
Wait your turn. Do it now, Do your own work, Stop chatting,
Share it, Take out your book, Put away your book, Pick up your
pencil, Open the windows, Do your homework, Show me your
books, etc.

S: 교사의 지시문을 들으며 동작을 따라한다.

T: Now, listen carefully what I say and make gestures.

S: 학생들은 교사의 지시를 구두로 따라하지 않고 동작을 취한다.

- words about classroom commands: Come up to the front, Go to the board,
Say it, Spell it, Write it, Take out your book, Put away your book, Ask/Answer
the question, Look at me/the board/the DVD/the screen, Listen to me/the
CD, Share it, Talk about/Discuss it, Help each other, Work alone/in a group.
Work with a partner/Work in pairs, Break up into small groups, Take one and
pass them on, Pass out the handouts, Pass them around, Correct the
mistakes, Hand in your homework, Look up the dictionary, Take notes,
Choose/Circle the correct answer, Cross out the odd one, Fill in the blank,

→ 〈Follow the Leader〉게임
- 가위, 바위, 보를 해서 이긴
사람이 취하는 동작을 모두가
동시에 따라하거나 리더가 동
작을 취하면 한 사람씩 이어서
따라하는 게임-으로 먼저 분
위기를 조성하는 것도 좋다.

Mark the answer/Bubble the answer, Match the words, Underline/Unscramble the word, Put the words in order, etc.

T: It was fun. Now it is your turn. One person gives instructions and we follow them. Who wants to start first? Yun goes first. Here we go.

S: 학생들은 한사람씩 돌아가며 지시를 내리고 나머지 학생들은 지시에 맞는 동작을 취한다.

Ending a Lesson

T: We talked about objects in the classroom, today. When you want to know something in English, you can ask, 'What's this in English?' or 'How do you say it in English?' Also we learned Konglish expressions are not English. Tell me some correct words we learned today.

S: A spiral notebook, an air conditioner, a cell phone.......

T: How do you say 'cheating' in Korean?

S: 커닝.

T: Is a sharppen English?

S: No.

T: Then how can we correct it?

S: A mechanical pencil

T: That's right. Bill showed his classroom in Canada and we compared classroom objects. We have a map but we don't have a globe. He has a big pencil sharpener in his classroom. We drew our ideal classrooms and talked about some essential objects we need. It was great you told the reasons. You showed you are very nice and kind. I was so touched.

T: Thank you for joining the class and see you next time.

S: Bye-bye.

➜배운 내용을 간략하게 정리해본다. 처음 수업을 할 때에는 교사의 말이 수업시간의 대부분을 차지하지만 학생들의 말하기가 익숙해지면 학생들이 학습한 내용을 정리하도록 한다.

To Better Teachers

⊃ Look around your classroom. Are there desks, chairs, pens, markers, spiral notebooks, textbooks, workbooks, pencils, pencil sharpeners and erasers? Is there chalk, notebook paper, a map, a chalkboard, a white board, a dictionary, a clock, a bookcase, a computer, an overhead projector, a DVD player, a stereo/CD player and a bulletin board? Why don't you describe your classroom in detail? Every single object counts. Also describe the ideal classroom you want. What is the big difference?

My Classroom vs. Ideal Classroom

_____

_____

_____

_____

⊃ What are your frequent instructions? Write down classroom commands you use.

_____

_____

_____

_____

⊃ Write down the meaning of each word. Try not to Konglish expressions.

1. blind date

2. omelet with/over rice

3. bottoms up

4. Sprite/7-Up

5. vomit/throw up

6. wakeup call

7. autograph/signature

8. (steering) wheel

9. window tinting

10. horn

11. convertible(car)

12. rear view mirror

13. mansion

14. studio apartment

15. apartment (house/building)

16. condominium

17. grocery store

18. (auto) repair shop

19. pool(billiards)

20. contact lens/contacts

21. permanent/perm

22. air conditioner

23. stereo

24. amateur

25. remote control/remote

26. cellular phone/mobile phone/cell phone

27. accelerator(British), gas pedal(America)

28. mass media/ the press

29. underwear(panties/briefs)

30. jacket

31. flip-flop/thong

32. hiking boots

33. student group/club

34. notebook

35. cut-off line

36. cream(coffee)

37. part time job

38. percent

39. TV advertisement /TV ad/commercial

40. sci-fi
41. bar
42. stapler
43. greenhouse
44. turtleneck
45. old maid
46. warranty
47. brand name
48. laminate
59. cast
50. Swiss Army knife

Small Talk
Conversation Etiquette

Goals	**Students can understand the etiquette of small talk.**
Questions	• What are good topics for small talk? • What are 'dos and don'ts' of small talk?
Task	• Students ask general questions and give answers. • Students make a list of small talk 'dos and don'ts'.
Teaching Aids	pictures/dolls of Tarzan & Jane, paper

Note

'Small Talk'는 가벼운 대화를 가리키는 말이다. 흔히 버스를 기다리거나 볼일을 보기 위해 대기 및 이동할 때 자주 사용된다. 따라서 깊이 있는 대화는 아니지만 경시할 수 없는 것이므로 이런 대화를 위해서는 어떤 주제가 좋은지 어떤 이야기를 하거나 하지 않는 것이 좋은지 이해할 수 있도록 한다.

Gist of a Lesson

Starting a Lesson		
▪ Greeting ▪ Routine Questions ▪ Checking Attendance ▪ Warm-Up	▪ 타잔과 제인 소개하기	● 그림/인형
Developing a Lesson		
▪ Presentation	▪ 타잔과 제인의 대화 1, 2 (small talk의 예를 보여준다.)	● 막대 인형
▪ Essential Question 1	▪ What are good topics for small talk? (가벼운 대화 주제로 좋은 것은 무엇일까요?)	● 그룹 활동
▪ Activity 1	▪ small talk로 좋은 주제와 나쁜 주제 목록 만들기 (그룹별로 목록을 만들어 서로 비교해 본다.)	● (큰) 종이
▪ Essential Question 2	▪ What are 'dos and don'ts' of small talk? (대화중에 지켜야할 예절에는 어떤 것이 있을까요?)	● 그룹 활동
▪ Activity 2	▪ 대화중에 지켜야할 예절의 목록 만들기 ('dos'와 'don'ts'로 나누어 목록을 작성한다.)	● (큰) 종이
Ending a Lesson		
▪ Wrap-Up	▪ 배운 내용 요약	

Teaching and Learning Plan

Starting a Lesson

T: Good morning, everyone.

S: Good morning, Teacher.

T: What's up? Anything new?

S: Nothing much.

T: It is getting warmer, isn't it?

S: Yes, it is.

T: Tell me the day and date, please.

S: It's Friday, April 7th.

T: Thanks. Is anyone missing?

S: No.

T: I'm happy to see you all.

T: (타잔 그림을 꺼내며) Do you know who he is?

S: He is Tarzan.

T: Right. He is Tarzan. He is from the jungle. He could not talk because he had animal friends only. Fortunately he met a friend. Her name is Jane.

T: (제인 그림을 꺼내며) Who is she?

S: She is Jane.

T: Right. This is Jane. She teaches Tarzan how to talk. Tarzan loves talking. When he talks, he is happy.

→늑대소년의 이야기를 들려 주면서 인간에게 있어서 언어의 소중함을 일깨워 주어도 좋다.

34

T: Do you think talking is important? 여러분은 말하는 것이 중요하다고 생각해요?

S: Yes, I do.

T: Why do we talk? 우리는 왜 말을 할까요?

S: 생각하는 것을 이야기하려고요.

T: You are very smart. We need to talk to show our thoughts, opinions, emotions, etc. and to understand others. We cannot live alone. We should connect ourselves with others. That's why we need to talk. Are you following me?

S: Yes, I am.

T: We can start the conversation with small talk. When you meet someone you don't know very well, you can make small talk. Now you will listen to several dialogs. Tell me what they talk about.

(교사는 타잔과 제인의 그림을 붙인 막대 인형을 가지고 역할극을 보여준다)

►Dialog 1◄

(Tarzan and Jane are waiting for a school bus.)

Tarzan: Hello. I'm Tarzan.

Jane: Hi, Tarzan. I'm Jane.

Tarzan: Nice to meet you, Jane. Where are you from?

Jane: I'm from Turkey. And you?

Tarzan: I'm from the jungles of Africa.

Jane: Wow, I hear it's wild and beautiful there.

Tarzan: Yes, it is. How long have you been in London?

Jane: For around two years.

Tarzan: Oh, look. It's going to rain soon.

Jane: Do you have an umbrella?

→small talk의 정의를 설명할 때 가장 좋은 것은 실제 대화를 보여주는 예문이다.

→대화1의 small talk
❶ 인사
❷ 이름
❸ 국적
❹ 날씨

Tarzan: No. But I love rain. I can take a shower with rain.

Jane: Then I'm sure you will like London. It has many rainy days.

Tarzan: That's great.

Tarzan and Jane exchange greetings, names and nationalities. Then they talk about the weather.

(활용 어휘)

- It is _____. There's going to be _____.
- words about weather: cool, freezing, clear, foggy/hazy, smoggy, humid, raining, drizzling, snowing, hailing, sleeting, lightening, thunder/snow/(yellow) dust storm, heat wave, etc.

Now listen to the second dialog.

►Dialog 2◄

(Tarzan and Jane make small talk before class begins.)

Tarzan: Hi.

Jane: Hello. Did you catch the news?

Tarzan: You mean the heavy rain in Seoul?

Jane: Yes. I heard roads and streets were filled with water.

Tarzan: I saw it on TV. It was terrible.

Jane: Buildings and bridges were broken.

Tarzan: Many people lost their home.

Jane: Some people were dead or missing.

Tarzan: Fortunately many volunteers gather to help them.

Jane: It is so touching.

Tarzan: I hope they overcome the situation.

Jane: I hope so.

T: What do they talk about?

S: They talk about news.

→대화 2의 small talk
❶ News
❷ Opinion

T: Right. News can be a good topic of small talk.

T: **"What are good topics for small talk?"** What are bad topics for small talk? Why don't you discuss them with your group members?

S: 학생들은 몇 개의 모둠으로 나뉘어 'small talk'에 무난하고 적절한 대화주제 및 좋지 않은 대화주제에 관해 이야기하고 목록을 작성한다.

➤교사는 그룹별로 작성한 목록을 게시하고 공통점과 차이점을 비교한 후 정리한다. 또한 적절한 대화주제 중에서 몇 가지를 선정하여 그와 관련된 대화를 학생들과 완성해보는 것도 좋은 활동이 된다.

T: So, for small talk you want to talk about schools, teachers, games, pets, entertainers, books, sports, clothes, movies, TV programs, hobbies etc. Some bad topics include parents' salaries, scores/academic records, negative comments about other people, rumors, appearance, etc. Are these what you said?

S: Yes, they are.

(**활용 어휘**)

- Do you have a pet? Yes. I have a _____. What's its name?
- words about pets: cat, kitten, dog, puppy, hamster, guinea pig, goldfish, canary, etc.
- I like your _____. Thank you.
- words about clothes: shirt, T-shirt, blouse, sweater, jacket, vest, pants, jeans, dress, uniform, shorts, overalls, coat, etc.
- I like him. He's a <u>tall</u> <u>thin</u> <u>middle-aged</u> <u>man</u> with <u>curly</u> <u>gray</u> <u>hair</u>.
- words about people: averaged height/short, heavy/average weight/slim, young/elderly, boy/girl/woman/senior citizen, straight/wavy/short/long/shoulder length, black/brown/blond/red/bald, etc.
- She is pregnant.
  He is physically challenged.
  She is hearing impaired.
  He is vision impaired.

➤사람이나 사물에 대해 기술할 때 사용하는 형용사는 반대 개념을 활용하여 익히도록 한다. 예를 들면, 'loose-tight, fast-slow, wide-narrow, neat-messy, smooth-rough', etc.

T: Now let's think about some 'dos and don'ts' during small talk. **"What are 'dos and don'ts' of small talk?"** 우리가 가벼운 대화중

에 해야 할 일과 하지 말아야할 일에는 어떤 것이 있을까요?

S: 대화중 지켜야할 예절에 대해 '해야 할 일'과 '하지 말아야 할 일'로 분류해 이야기하면서 목록을 작성한다.

T: 그룹의 목록을 모아 전체 목록을 작성한다.

Here are dos and don'ts of small talk you discussed.

Dos

- Smile.
- Use eye contact.
- Be a better listener than a speaker.
- Speak clearly.
- Be ready to stop your topic/talking.
- Choose the topic to suit others' interests.
- Let the speaker finish his or her story.
- Be positive.
- Enjoy humor.
- Try to find good points of others.

Don'ts

- Do not cross arms and legs.
- Do not look around.
- Do not check phones(text or time).
- Do not murmur.
- Do not make a 3-minute conversation turn into 30 minutes.
- Do not change the topic to suit your own interest.
- Do not curse or swear.
- Do not be negative.

T: Any comments?

S: I am happy to learn the etiquette of small talk.

T: That is good.

➤교사는 small talk주제로 좋은 것과 그렇지 못한 것, 대화 중에 해야 할 일과 하지 말아야할 일을 'the etiquette of small talk'로 묶어서 교실에 게시하거나 인쇄해서 나누어 주도록 한다.

T: We are people living together. To show our thoughts and emotions, and to understand others' opinions and feelings, we talk.

We can start a conversation with small talk. There are some good topics for small talk. We can talk about weather, news, subjects, homework, pets, sports, hobbies, etc. If the topics of small talk are too personal and offensive to others, we'd better not start. Hope you understood the etiquette of small talk.

You did a good job. Have a good day.

S: Bye.

➤교사는 'Global Etiquette'을 조사해 오는 과제를 줄 수 있다.

'침묵은 금이다'라는 말은 영어(언어)를 공부하는데 도움이 되는 것 같지는 않다. 영어권 사람과 대화를 할 때 영어가 어색하고 자연스럽게 구사되지 않아 (체면과 예의를 운운하며) 아무 말도 하지 않는 것보다는 오히려 실수하더라도 말을 하는 편이 낫다. 무례한 사람이 되고 싶지 않다면 말이다.

Small Talk(가벼운 대화)는 특정 상황에서 당연하고도 자연스러운 비격식의 대화로 서먹서먹한 분위기나 어색한 침묵을 깨는데 사용된다. 이러한 Small Talk에는 특정한 화제(topic of conversation) 가 있다. Small Talk는 누가 무엇을 언제 어디에서 그리고 왜 사용하는지 생각해보고 가벼운 대화 속에 등장하는 몇 가지 표현을 살펴보자.

Who?
Small Talk는 잘 알지 못하는 사람들, 즉 그냥 아는 사람들(just acquaintances)—예를 들면 같은 직장에 근무하는 사람, 같은 아파트나 마을에 사는 사람 및 각종 서비스를 제공하는 사람들—과 나누는 대화이다.

What?
가장 빈번히 사용되는 화제는 날씨(weather)이다. 날씨는 대화를 시작하기에 가장 무난한 주제가 된다. 그다음으로 무난한 것은 시사(current events)이다. 논란의 소지가 큰 것이 아니라면 뉴스에 대한 이야기를 하면 된다. 스포츠는 (국가전이 있을 때는 더욱) 좋은 화제가 되며 유명 인사나 연예계 인물에 대한 소식도 대화를 이끌어내는 소재가 된다. 또한 대화를 하는 사람들이 (같은 곳에 근무한다든가 같은 지역이나 아파트에 거주하는 등의) 공통점을 지니고 있을 때 이 또한 좋은 화제가 된다.

  Small Talk로 바람직하지 않은 것은 연봉이나 가정사 같은 너무나 사적인 정보에 관해 대화를 시도하는 것이며 의상이나 머리스타일에 대한 칭찬은 괜찮지만 신체(body)에 대해서는 아무리 칭찬이라 하더라도 언급하지 않도록 한다. 또한 다른 사람에 대한 부정적인 말은 하지 않도록 한다. 여러분이 이야기하는 사람의 친구가 바로 당신의 말을 듣고 있는 사람일 수도 있다. 또한 청자가 어떤 사람인지 모르기 때문에 당신 자신에 대한 비밀이나 사적인 정보와 같은 개인적 화제는 삼가도록 한다. 종교(religion)나 정치(politics)와 같이 논쟁의 소지가 많은 문제에 대해서도 언급하지 않는 것이 좋으며 다른 사람이 불편해하거나 관심이 없는 문제에 대해서는 더 이상 이야기하지 않는 것이 현명하다.

Where?
Small Talk는 어느 곳에서든지 할 수 있으나 주로 사람들이 무엇인가를 기다리는 곳에서 자주 발생한다. 예를 들어 여러분 곁에서 버스나 기차 및 비행기를 기다리고 있는 다른 사람과 이야기를 주고받거나 병원이나 은행 등에서 자신의 차례를 기다릴 때에도 small talk를 시도할 수 있다. 특히 각종 모임과 같은 사교 행사(social events)에서는 참석한 사람들과 어우러져 small talk를 하는 것이 필수적이다.

When?
대화를 시작하는 시점은 누군가를 처음 만났을 때인데, 예를 들어 직장동료를 만났을 때 인사를 하고 나서 바로 날씨에 관해 이야기할 수 있다. 하지만 그 동료를 다시 만나게 되면 단지 눈인사만으로 충분하다. 또한 주변이 조용할 때에는 가벼운 대화(a casual conversation)를 시작하는데 적기이며 누군가 여러분을 보고 (미소와 눈인사 같은) 표시를 주면 대화를 시작하도록 한다. 쉬는 시간이나 점심시간도 말을 걸기에 좋은 때이다.

날씨와 같은 가벼운 대화를 시도하고자 주변에서 진지하게 이야기하고 있는 사람들의 대화를 방해(중단) 하면 안 된다. 또한 책이나 신문을 보고 있는 사람에게 말을 거는 것도 좋지 않다.

무엇보다 중요한 것은 대화를 시작하고 나서 이제 그만 이야기하고 싶다는 신호를 빨리 알아채고 대화를 끝내는 것이다.

Why?

가벼운 대화를 시도하는 이유는 다양하지만 무엇인가를 기다릴 때 말을 거는 것이 보편적인 것을 보면 불편한 침묵(uncomfortable silence)을 깨고 시간을 때우는 데 있다. 어떤 사람들은 예의를 지키기 위해 대화를 시도하는데, 가령 모임에 참석해서 다른 사람들과 어울리고 싶지 않다고 구석에 혼자 앉아있는 것은 무례한 행동이 된다. 또한 다른 사람을 소개받았을 때에도 예의바른 관심을 보여주기 위해서 small talk를 시작한다.

〈Small Talk(Conversation Starters)에 자주 등장하는 표현〉

Talking about the weather(날씨에 관해 이야기 할 때)

- Beautiful day/Awful day, isn't it?
- Perfect day, isn't it? Did you order this sunshine?
- We couldn't ask for a nicer day, could we?
- It looks like it's going to rain.
- I hear they're <u>calling for</u> thunderstorms all weekend. (→일기예보에서 ~한 날씨를 예상하다.)

Talking about current events(뉴스에 관해 이야기 할 때)

- Did you catch the news today?
- Did you hear about torrential flooding and landslides?
- I read in the paper today that volunteers gathered to clean up water damage.
- I heard on the radio today that Kim won the gold medal.

At work & At a social event(직장이나 사교 모임에서)

- Have you worked here long?
- You look like you could <u>use</u> a cup of coffee. (→마시고 싶다)
- What do you think of the new equipment?

- I love your dress. It suits you very well.

- Pretty nice place, huh?

- Are you enjoying yourself?

Waiting somewhere(어딘가에서 기다리고 있을 때)

- I didn't think it would be so busy today.

- The bus must be running late today.

- It looks like we are going to be here a while.

- How old's your baby? She is so cute.

- How long have you been waiting?

- The trees are beautiful at this time of year, aren't they?

⊃ Are the following statements True or False?

1. One reason people use small talk is to eliminate an uncomfortable silence.

2. It is common to use small talk when you are waiting in a long line-up.

3. It is common to discuss the weather in an elevator.

4. During small talk with a stranger, it is not common to discuss personal information relating to work.

5. Sport is not a safe topic when making small talk.

6. Politics is a controversial subject according to society.

7. Religion is a safe topic when making small talk.

8. Private information about one's personal life is not acceptable.

9. Though one is obviously not interested in the subject, you should continue with that subject.

10. Keeping negative comments out of your small talk is recommendable.

11. It is inappropriate to make small talk with your mail carrier or delivery person.

12. It is rude for both children and adults not to make small talk with strangers.

13. One should never compliment another person's clothes in order to make small talk.

14. It is rude to interrupt a conversation in order to make small talk.

15. When one suggests ending the conversation, you should take the hint and stop talking.

16. It is not appropriate to discuss salaries.

Answers: T, T, T, T, F, T, F, T, F, T, F, F, F, F, T, T, T

Numbers
Numbers Around Us

Goals	**Students can understand the importance of numbers in their daily lives.**
Questions	• What would happen if there were no numbers? • When do you use numbers?
Task	• Students talk about situations that need numbers. • Students complete invitation letters.
Teaching Aids	calendar, clock, objects with numbers, invitation card, cellular(phone), paper

Note

'1~100, 1~1000 혹은 1~10,000'까지의 숫자를 세어보거나 'one-first, two-second, three-third'처럼 기수와 서수를 연결하여 아무런 맥락 없이 기계적으로 암기하는 것보다는 일상생활 속에서 숫자를 사용하는 경우(시간, 전화 번호, 돈, 날짜 등)를 떠올리며 숫자가 얼마나 중요한지 왜 알아두어야 하는지를 이해하도록 한다.

Gist of a Lesson

Starting a Lesson		
<ul><li>Greeting</li><li>Routine Questions</li><li>Checking Attendance</li><li>Warm-Up</li></ul>	▪ 숫자가 없는 달력 보여주기	● 달력
Developing a Lesson		
▪ Presentation	▪ 숫자가 있는 실물이나 그림 보여주기 (우리 주변에 있는 숫자 찾아보기)	● 실물/그림
▪ Essential Question 1	▪ What would happen if there were no numbers? (숫자가 없다면 어떻게 될까요?)	● 개별 응답
▪ Activity 1	▪ 시계와 전화기에 숫자가 없다면 어떤 일이 일어날까? (그룹별로 시계와 전화가 없는 상황을 이야기 해 본다.)	● 그룹 활동
▪ Essential Question 2	▪ When do you use numbers? (그룹별로 숫자를 사용하는 상황을 목록으로 만든다.)	● 그룹 활동 (큰) 종이
▪ Storytelling	▪ '생일 파티 초대장' 이야기 (날짜와 시간이 빠진 초대장을 받고 전화를 걸어 확인)	● 초대장/ 전화기
▪ Activity 2	▪ 초대장 완성하기 (빈칸을 채워 초대장을 완성한다.)	● 빈 초대장
Ending a Lesson		
▪ Wrap-Up	▪ 배운 내용 요약	

Teaching and Learning Plan

Starting a Lesson

T: Hello, everyone.

S: Hello, Teacher.

T: How are you doing? Pretty good?

S: Yes.

T: Good. Very good.

T: Look outside. What's the weather like today?

S: It is cloudy.

T: It seems to rain soon. Tell me what day it is today.

S: It's Friday.

T: TGI Friday! Thank God. It's Friday. What's the date today?

S: Today is.......

T: Let me show you a calendar (숫자가 없는 달력을 꺼낸다).
Oh, there is no numbers. Can you tell me the date?

S: No, I can't.

T: You're right. We cannot say the day or the date, because this
calendar has no numbers on it. It is very strange, isn't it?

Developing a Lesson

T: Look around you. What has numbers? (시계를 보여주며) My
watch has numbers. What else has numbers?

S: Phones, clocks, books, money.......

T: You said books?

S: Yes. There are page numbers.

T: I see. And the volume numbers.
(주변의 사물이나 그림을 가리키며) cell phones, clocks, money,
books(pages), calendars, mathematics text books, receipts, bills,

➤숫자가 적혀있는 사물은 주
변에서 쉽게 구할 수 있다.

45

addresses, etc.

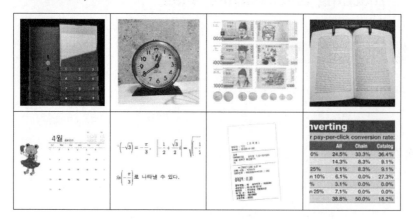

T: Wow, we have lots of things that have numbers.

But what would happen if there were no numbers like this calendar? (숫자가 없는 달력을 보여준다.) Can you tell me **"What would happen if there were no numbers?"**

S: 수를 셀 수가 없어요.

T: We couldn't count.

S: We can't call.

T: Right. We couldn't make a phonecall because the phone had no numbers.

S: 시험을 치를 필요가 없어요.

T: That is good, isn't it? Though we took a test, there would be no scores. We would not need to take tests.

S: 숫자가 없으면 물건을 사고 팔 수 없어요.

T: Without numbers, We can't buy or sell things.

S: There is no banks, post offices, shops, etc.

T: We cannot take buses or trains.

S: We can't use computers.

T: We can't make an appointment to meet someone.

T: (숫자가 없는 시계를 보여주며) Look at this clock. What time is it? Can you tell me the time?

S: No.

T: No, you can't. You cannot answer because there are no numbers.

→숫자가 없다면 어떤 일이 발생할지 상상하여 자유롭게 이야기할 수 있도록 분위기를 만들고 학생들의 한국어 답변은 영어로 바꾸어준다.

→digital clock

The clock is useless without numbers. What would happen if there were no numbers on the clock?

S: 시계에 숫자가 없을 경우 어떤 일이 일어날 수 있는지 친구들과 함께 이야기 한다.

T: Also talk about what would happen if there were no numbers on the phone/cellular phone? (전화기/휴대전화기를 보여준다.)

S: 전화기에 번호가 없을 경우 어떤 일이 일어날 수 있는지 친구들과 이야기 한다.

T: Now talk about some situations we need numbers. **"When do we use numbers?"** 숫자는 언제 사용하나요? Then make a list of those situations.

S: 일상생활에서 숫자가 필요한 상황―언제 그리고 왜 숫자를 사용하는가―을 상의하고 목록을 작성한다.

T: 그룹을 돌며 숫자로 답을 해야 하는 질문을 던진다.

→숫자가 필요한 상황을 이야기 하고 간단하게 목록을 작성한다. 숫자에는 기수와 서수가 포함된다.

활용 구문

- How old are you? I'm _____ years old.
- What's the temperature? It's _____ degrees Celsius/Centigrade.
- How many students are there in your class? There are _____.
- How many people are there in your family/Korea/this city? _____.
- What floor do you live on? I live on the _____ floor.
- What grade are you in? I'm in the _____ grade.
- What time do you get up? (schedule) I get up at _____.
- How much is it? It is _____ dollars/cents/won.
- When is your birthday? What is your date of birth?
  I was born _____(month)_____(day), _____(year).

T: Now we can understand how important the numbers are.
Yesterday I got an invitation card. Let me see. It is from Jack.
(초대장을 가지고 아이들에게 이야기를 들려준다.)
Oh, no! I want to join the party, but I can't. There is no date and no time. What should I do?(동작을 취한다)

Dear Teacher

Hello. This is Jack.

Sunday is my birthday. There is a birthday party at my house. My house is at 17 Jongno street. You can enjoy good music and delicious food. Please come and have some fun. See you then. Bye

Jack

P.S. Could you reply(RSVP) by phone? My phone number is 010-2345-6789.

S: Call him.

T: Thank you. I have Jack's phone number. Here is my phone. Let's call him up(동작을 취한다). Hello. This is Teacher. Can I talk to Jack? Oh, hi Jack. Thank you for sending me an invitation card. I want to join the party. Can you tell me the date and time? Uh-huh. 6 pm on March 10? Okay. See you then. Bye.

T: I knew it. Look at this calendar, everyone. Let's mark March 10th on the calendar, together. (달력을 넘기며) January, February, and March! Here it is. (숫자를 짚어가며) First, second, third, fourth, fifth, sixth, seventh, eighth, ninth and tenth. Circle the number 10. Jack's birthday is March 10th. Also look at this clock. (시계바늘을 돌리며) One, two, three, four, five and six. Good. Now I can join the party.

T: Well, Sujin when is your birthday?

S: January 20th.

T: 달력을 넘겨 날짜에 동그라미 한다. Sujin이 다른 친구에게 생일을 물어보도록 한다.

➔ 학생들이 생일을 이야기하면 바로 달력을 넘겨 표시하고, 예를 들어 5월 18일일 경우 May 18th를 두세 번 반복하도록 한다. 1st~31st 혹은 100th까지 먼저 연습시키는 것 보다 본인에게 의미 있는 날짜를 기억하도록 한다.

S: Danny, when is your birthday?

S: December 15th.

T: (학생들의 답변이 끝나고 다음 활동을 시작하기 전에 챈트를 한다.)

Let's chant together.

January-February-March ❢ ❢ April-May-June ❢ ❢

July-August-September ❢ ❢ October-November-December ❢ ❢

T: How about making an invitation letter like Jack?

Think about who you want to invite and when you have a birthday party.

Please get one and pass around the handouts.

Let's look at the letter.

Can you see the blanks? You can fill in the blanks.

S: 아래의 초대장에 빈칸을 채워 자신만의 초대장을 완성한다.

Dear (the person you want to invite)

Hello.
This is(your name/nickname).
(Month) (date) is my birthday. It is(day). There is a
birthday party at my house at (time). Can you come to my
house? Please let me know. Call me at (phone number). My
address is( ).

Warm wishes,
(your name/nickname)

> Ending a Lesson

T: Today we found the numbers around us are very(very) important.

We use numbers to say date, time, address, phones, grade, class, buying and selling something, and so on. Without numbers, our lives may be complicated and messy. Thank for your enthusiasm for class. Have a nice day.

S: Bye.

다음에 맞도록 구체적인 교수 학습 활동을 구상해볼 수도 있다.

Topic. Numbers

Goals	**Students can understand the difference between cardinal and ordinal numbers.**
Questions	When do we use cardinal numbers like one, two, three, etc.? When do we use ordinal numbers such as first, second, third, etc.?
Task	Students measure the pencils and compare the length of them. Students arrange the pencils according to the length and tell the order.
Teaching -Learning Activities	1. A teacher shows some cardinal numbers and the situations they are used. 2. A teacher recasts what the students say(if they say in mother tongue) in English. 3. Students discuss the situations cardinal and ordinal numbers are used.

1. 숫자는 우리 일상생활에서 빠질 수 없는 중요한 요소 중 하나이다. 숫자에는 기수와 서수가 있다. 기수는 수를 나타내는데 기초가 되는 수로 0에서 9까지의 정수를 일컫고, 서수는 순서나 차례를 나타내는 수를 말한다.

0	-zero,
10	-ten,
100	-one hundred,
1,000	-one thousand,
10,000	-ten thousand,
100,000	-one hundred thousand,
1,000,000	-one million,
1,000,000,000	-one billion

1¢	-one cent/penny
5¢	-five cents/nickel
10¢	-ten cents/dime
25¢	-twenty-five cents/quarter
50¢	-fifty cents/half dollar

(kinds of dollar bills: one/five/ten/twenty/fifty/one hundred-dollar bill)

$1.40	-a dollar (and) forty (cents)
$17.90	-seventeen (dollars) (and) ninety (cents)

2:30	-half past two/two thirty
6:15	-a quarter after six/six fifteen
8:45	-a quarter to nine/eight forty-five

0.75	-(zero) point seven five
20.468	-twenty point four six eight
55%	-fifty-five percent
25℃	-twenty-five degrees Celsius/Centigrade
90℉	-ninety degrees Fahrenheit

1/2	-a half

1/3, 2/3	-one third, two thirds
1/4, 3/4	-one quarter, three quarters
21st	-twenty-first
42nd	-forty-second
33rd	-thirty-third
79th	-seventy-ninth
100th	-one hundredth

2. 다음에 해당하는 예문을 다섯 개씩 들어보시오.

1. Time(시간)

2. Date(날짜)

3. Money(돈)

4. Number(개수)

5. Telephone Number(전화번호)

6. Address(주소)

7. Measurement(측정)

8. Age(나이)

9. Temperature(기온)

10. Rank & Order(순위와 순서)

3. 다음을 참고하여 특별한 날, 기념일, 생일, 명절, 축제의 날짜를 쓰시오.

1) January: New Year's Day, Lunar New Year's Day(음력설)
2) February: Graduation Ceremony, St. Valentine's Day
3) March: Independence Movement Day(3 · 1절), Entrance Ceremony
4) April: April Fool's Day(만우절), Arbor Day(식목일)
5) May: Coming-of-Age Day(성년의 날), Buddha's Birthday(석가탄신일), Children's Day, Parents' Day, Teachers' Day

6) June: Memorial Day(현충일)

7) July: Constitution Day(제헌절), Dog Days/dog days of summer(복날)

8) August: Independence Day(광복절), summer vacation(여름방학)

9) September: going back to school(개학), chuseok/Hangawi(추석/한가위)

10) October: National Foundation Day(개천절), *Hangeul* Proclamation Day(한글날)

11) November: Students' Day(학생의 날)

12) December: Christmas Day, New Year's Eve, Winter Vacation

Mr. Moon and Miss Sun

Goals	
Questions	
Task	
Teaching Aids	

Note

Gist of a Lesson

Starting a Lesson		
▪ Greeting ▪ Warm-Up		
Developing a Lesson		
▪ Activity 1 ▪ Essential Question 1 ▪ Essential Question 2 ▪ Activity 2 ▪ Essential Question 3 ▪ Essential Question 4 ▪ Activity 3		
Ending a Lesson		
▪ Wrap-Up		

Scene 1

A long time ago, there lived a little brother and a sister with their mother deep in the woods. They were poor but they were happy all the time. One day, their mother went to another village to help prepare for a great party. The children had to stay home alone and watch over the house.

My story

The sky had already become dark when the mother started out for home. Suddenly a big tiger appeared and roared. "If you give me one rice cake, I won't eat you," said the tiger. Too frightened, she threw the tiger a rice cake and started to run. The tiger ate it in one swallow and chased the mother.

My story

Scene 3

Before the mother reached the next hill, the tiger had already gotten there and said, "If you give me one rice cake, I won't eat you." The poor mother threw one rice cake and ran for the next hill. The tiger swallowed it at once and raced ahead of her. At each hill he waited for her and got the rice cake. Before long she had given the tiger the last rice cake. The tiger growled, "If you give me one rice cake, I won't eat you." But she had no more to give, and the tiger ate her up.

My story

It got darker and darker and finally it was night. The children were very worried, but still their mother didn't come home. Just at the moment, they heard a voice saying, "Children, mommy's home. Open the door." "That doesn't sound like my mom," said the boy. "I caught a cold and my throat is sore," said the voice from outside. "Show me your hand, then," shouted the boy. The tiger pushed a big, shaggy, clawed paw through the paper window. "That's not mom's hand," cried the little girl.

My story

Scene 5

The voice outside said, "I have worked very hard today. That's why my hands are all rough. Anyway you must be very hungry. I'll make you supper shortly." The tiger hurried into the kitchen and rattled the dishes, pretending to cook supper. When they peeped out through the hole in the paper window, they saw a tiger's tail come from Mother's clothes.

My story

Scene 6

Trying to calm down, the boy led his little sister outside quickly and calmly. They climbed a tree in the backyard. Back inside the house, the tiger was looking for the two children, running through the house. Finally the tiger saw them in the tree and set about climbing the tree. But, everytime he got halfway up the tree trunk, he slipped back down to the ground. The boy shouted, "Get some sesame oil and rub it all over the trunk." The tiger did exactly as he was told but the trunk was even more slippery than before.

My story

The girl could not help laughing, "You silly idiot! You can use an ax." Before the little girl realized her mistake, the tiger found an ax and struck the tree. He climbed higher and higher up the tree using the cuts. The children trembled with fear and prayed, "Oh, God, please send us a strong rope to save us." Just as they asked, a rope dropped gently down from the sky above. They grabbed the rope and were pulled up away into the sky.

My story

Scene 8

The tiger was angry and he prayed, "Oh God, send me a strong rope, too." Another rope dropped and he grabbed on. But the rope was rotten and snapped, sending the tiger falling to the ground below. The two children kept going higher and higher. The boy became the Sun and the girl became the Moon. But she was frightened at night. Her brother changed places with her and became the Moon. Ever since that day, no one could see her face directly because the shy Sun was brighter than anything else.

My story

Colors
What colors make you happy?

Goals	**Students can understand colors have meanings.**
Questions	• What does the color red (usually) stand for? • What color makes you happy?
Task	• Students draw Taegukgi and make their own flags. • Students talk about the emotions of colors.
Teaching Aids	national flags, traffic light, color pencils(color paper)

Note

무지개색이라 불리는 기본적인 색상의 이름을 암기하는데 그치지 않도록 한다.

Q. What color is it?   A. It's red/orange/yellow/green/blue/indigo/purple.

일상생활에서 위와 같은 대화를 주고받는 경우는 드물기 때문에, 어떤 경우에 '색깔'과 그와 관련된 표현이 사용되는지 생각해 본다. 색깔에는 의미와 감정이 담길 수 있음을 이해한다.

Gist of a Lesson

Starting a Lesson		
▪ Greeting ▪ Routine Questions ▪ Checking Attendance ▪ Warm-Up	▪ 의상, 신호등 색깔의 느낌과 의미 이야기하기	● 신호등
Developing a Lesson		
▪ Essential Question 1 ▪ Activity 1 ▪ Activity 2 ▪ Essential Question 2 ▪ Activity 3	▪ What does the color red stand for? (빨간 색은 어떤 의미가 있을까요?) ▪ 태극기에 있는 색깔의 의미 알고 그려보기 (태극기에 담긴 의미를 이해하고 직접 그려본다.) ▪ 무인도에 새로운 나라를 만든다면? (그룹별로 자신의 나라를 상징하는 국기를 만든 다.) ▪ What color makes you happy? (보면 기분 좋은 색깔에 대해 이야기한다.) ▪ 대화 완성하기 (색깔과 감정 어휘를 활용하여 대화 연습을 한다.)	● 개별 응답 ● 태극기/ 색연필 ● 색종이/ 색연필 ● 그룹 활동 ● 짝 활동
Ending a Lesson		
▪ Wrap-Up	▪ 배운 내용 요약	

Teaching and Learning Plan

Starting a Lesson

T: Good morning, everyone.

S: Good morning, Teacher.

T: Is everything going okay?

S: Yes it is.

T: Good. Look outside. What a beautiful day, isn't it?

S: Yes, it is.

T: Now would you look at me? How do I look today? Do I look good in red?

S: Yes, you do.

T: Thank you. Red is my favorite color. It makes me happy.

T: (신호등 사진을 보여주며) This is a traffic light. There are three colors. They are red, orange and green. What does red mean?

S: Stop.

T: It means 'stop'. How about orange?

S: Don't cross. Wait.

T: Right. The color orange means 'wait' and the color green eans 'go.' Colors have meanings I guess.

Developing a Lesson

T: Can you tell me something red? What is red?

S: Fire engines, apples, strawberries, tomatoes, watermelons, etc.

T: (응답을 반복해준다.) Fire engines are red.

- fire, blood, roses, heart, red cross(적십자), apples, strawberries, cherries, etc. (단복수를 구별해서 be동사에 주의한다.)

T: Then why are fire engines red? It could be white.

S: 응답한다.

T: The color red is easy to recognize. It tells something urgent. When we see the red fire engines, we help them move quickly to put out the fire and save people. That's why red is better for fire engines than white.

T: **"What does the color red (usually) stand for?"**

S: 응답한다.

T: It could mean 'hot', 'dangerous', 'important', 'beautiful', 'urgent', etc.

T: How about white? What has the color white?

S: 응답한다.

T: (응답을 반복해준다.) Snow is white.

- snowman, ice, polar bears, flour, rice, cheery blossoms, thread, magnolias, chrysanthemums, etc. (단복수를 구별해서 be동사에 주의한다.)

T: What does the color white stand for?

S: 응답한다.

T: It means 'pure', 'clean', 'cold', 'calm', 'sad', 'lonely', 'hopeful', 'peaceful', 'quiet' etc. As you said, the color white can mean lots of things.

T: (태극기를 보여주며) Do you know what it is? This is our national flag, Taegukgi/Taegeukgi. Here are some colors. What

➡교사는 아이들이 원하는 색상(빨강이 아니더라도)을 선택해서 그 색상을 가지고 있는 주변의 사물을 토대로 그 색상이 의미하는 것을 이야기하도록 한다.

66

color is the background?

S: It is white.

T: The color white means 'purity/cleanliness' and 'peace loving people'. Look at the center. What colors can you see?

S: Red and blue are in the center.

T: Red means the positive energy or masculine energy. Blue means the negative energy or feminine energy. The circle means the harmony of red and blue. Taeguk symbolizes the harmony of the universe. Also four trigrams represent heaven, earth, sun and moon. So Taegukgi shows the universe itself. Can you draw Taegukgi?

S: 태극기를 그리고 색칠해 본다.

➡태극기의 밑그림을 준비하여 색깔을 칠하도록 하거나 흰 종이에 직접 그려보도록 한다.

활용 어휘

- One black trigram is in each corner of the flag. ☰(geon) means heaven/east/spring, ☷(gon) means earth/west/summer, ☲(ri) means sun/south/fall and ☵(gam) means moon/north/winter.

T: Now look at this picture. How many colors can you see? Three. They are white, red and blue. 50 white stars mean 50 states, and red and white stripes mean 13 states in early days. Can you tell me the country?

S: U.S.A.

➡다른 여러 나라 국기 속에 있는 색깔과 그 색깔의 의미를 미리 조사해서 그룹별로 발표하는 시간을 갖는 것도 좋다.

✔ 다른 나라의 국기를 몇 개 더 보여주고 색깔을 이야기해보고 어떤 나라의 국기인지 맞춰 보도록 한다. 또한 국기의 공통점과 그 이유에 대해서도 생각해 보도록 한다.

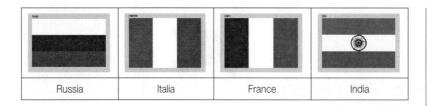

| Russia | Italia | France | India |

→그룹별로 무인도에 나라를 세운다고 생각하고 여러 가지 색깔을 사용하여 국기를 만든다.

T: Now imagine you found a deserted island. It is your own country. You need a flag for your country. Can you draw and color it? When you're done, you can describe the flag.

S: 무인도를 발견하여 자신의 나라를 만들고 그 나라를 상징하는 국기를 만들어 본다. 국기 안에 담겨 있는 모양과 색상이 무엇을 의미하는지 설명한다.

T: You did a good job.

Do you remember what my favorite color is?

S: Red.

T: That's right. Thank you for remembering it.

I love red. When I see red, it makes me happy. I feel confident and passionate/enthusiastic/powerful. How about you? **"What color makes you happy?"** Or What color makes you sad? How do you feel when you see red/yellow/blue?

S: 자신을 기분 좋고 행복하게 하거나 우울하고 슬프게 하는 색깔 및 특정 색상을 보았을 때 어떤 기분이 드는지 친구들과 이야기를 나눈다.

→활용 구문과 어휘를 사용해서 대화를 완성해 본다.

> ### 활용 구문 및 어휘

- **A:** How do you feel when you see _____(colors)?
  B: I feel _____(emotions) when I see _____(colors).
  _____(colors) makes me _____(emotions).
- colors: indigo blue, light blue, aquamarine, turquoise, dark green, grass green, olive green, apple green, yellow, orange, red, scarlet, light peach, peach, ochre, brown, umber, pink, violet, violet blue, black, white, gray, ivory, etc.
- emotions: happy, excited, proud, angry/mad, annoyed, furious, upset,

sad/unhappy, lonely, miserable, homesick, embarrassed, nervous, worried, surprised/shocked, scared/afraid, disappointed, frustrated, jealous, confused, bored, etc.

Ending a Lesson

T: We have many colors around us. Those colors are originally from the nature. In the society we live, each color has different meanings. Those meanings may be a little different from those in other countries, but there are some common meanings. For example, what does the color red stand for?

S: Hot, danger, warning, war, hatred, etc.

T: The color red symbolizes 'danger', 'fire', 'heat', 'blood', 'war', etc.

How do you feel when you see the color red?

S: I feel scared. I feel happy. I feel excited.

T: Good. In my case, the color red makes me happy. When I see red, I feel confident and passionate. Colors have meanings and in particular situations we should understand what they mean. Right?

S: Yes.

T: Did you enjoy the class? Thank you. See you next time.

S: Thank you. Bye.

1. Write down the following colors in English.

푸른빛 회색		회색빛 파랑	
칙칙한 회색		감청색	
은색		짙은 남색	
설백(순백)의		보라(청자색)	
회색 띤 연푸른색		연보라색	
하늘빛		자주색	
하늘색의		진홍색	
남옥, 담청록색		강한 분홍색	
청록색, 터키옥색		짙은 보라색	
선황색/진황색		남색	
황갈색		연어살빛	
낙타색/베이지색		산홋빛	
상아색		적갈색	
카키색(황갈색)		밤색, 고동색	
엷은 자주색		초콜릿색	
붉은 색이 도는 황색(비스크)		황갈색, 시에나색	
청록색		금빛	
강청색의		연두색	
녹색		옥색	

➡ Shades of Green: grass green, lime green, spring green, sea green, forest green, olive green

그밖에 '어두운'은 **dark**, '밝은'은 **light**, '짙은'은 **deep**, 그리고 '엷은'은 **pale**을 위의 색상 앞에 붙인다.

⟨Answers⟩

Slate Gray, Dim Gray, Silver, Snow-White, Alice Blue, Azure, Sky-Blue, Aquamarine, Turquoise, Goldenrod, Tan, Beige, Ivory, Khaki, Lavender, Bisque,

Cyan, Steel-Blue, Green, Slate Blue, Royal Blue, Navy, Violet, Orchid, Purple, Crimson, Hot Pink, Plum(Deep Purple), Indigo, Salmon, Coral, Auburn, Maroon, Chocolate, Sienna, Gold, Chartreuse, Aqua

2. Practice the following dialog filling the blanks.

A: I like your _____(colors) _____(clothes).

You look good in _____(colors).

B: Thank you. _____ is my favorite color.

I need _____(clothes). What color do you recommend?

A: How about _____(colors)?

✓ Clothes: blouse, tunic, shirt, T-shirt, vest, jacket, parka, coat, trench coat, sweater, pullover, turtleneck, cap, hat, skirt, pants/jeans, shorts, leggings, tights, dress, (evening) gown, suit, overalls, tie, scarf, etc.

3. You are going to color the following bags. Which color is good for each one?

Shapes
Shapes have functions.

Goals	**Students can understand containers have different shapes and functions.**
Questions	• When and why do we need containers? • What kinds of containers do you use?
Task	• Students talk about why or when they need containers. • Students describe containers they use and design a new container.
Teaching Aids	box, containers(bottle, egg carton, package, can, etc.) or the picture of containers

Note

모양의 이름을 가르치는 것은 궁극적 목표—일상생활에서 그 모양을 가지고 있는 것에는 어떤 것이 있으며 왜 그런 모양을 가지고 있는지를 이해—를 실현하기 위한 전체의 일부분이 되어야 한다. 즉 'Shape'이라는 주제를 가지고 circle(원), triangle(사각형), diamond(마름모), square(정사각형), rectangle(직사각형), star(별), heart(하트) 등의 이름을 아는 것에만 국한시키지 않는다.

Gist of a Lesson

Starting a Lesson		
▪ Greeting ▪ Routine Questions ▪ Checking Attendance ▪ Warm-Up	▪ 여러 가지 용기가 담기 상자 보여주기	● 상자
Developing a Lesson		
▪ Presentation	▪ 상자 안의 용기 소개 (bottle of water, package of cookies, carton of eggs)	● 용기
▪ Essential Question 1	▪ When and why do we need containers? (언제 그리고 왜 용기가 필요할까요?)	● 그룹 활동
▪ Essential question 2	▪ What kinds of containers do you use? (여러분은 어떤 용기를 사용하나요?)	● 그룹 활동
▪ Activity 1	▪ 모양의 기능을 이해하고 내가 사용하는 용기 그려보기 (그 용기를 언제 왜 사용하는지 이야기한다.)	● 개별 활동
▪ Activity 2	▪ 평소에 생각했거나 앞으로 필요한 용기 디자인하기 (야채 용기, 산소를 담는 용기, 등)	● 그룹 활동
Ending a Lesson		
▪ Wrap-Up	▪ 배운 내용 요약	

Teaching and Learning Plan

Starting a Lesson

T: Hello, everyone.

S: Hello, Teacher.

T: How are you doing?

S: Very well. Thank you.

T: Look outside. How's the weather today?

S: It's cloudy.

T: Can you tell me what day it is today?

S: It's Wednesday.

T: What's the date today?

S: It's May 20th.

T: Is anyone missing?

S: No one is missing.

T: Thank you. I'm so happy to see you all. Your English is getting better day by day.

T: Today I brought a box. Can you guess what is inside? I'll give you a hint. You are running outside now. You are out of breath(숨을 헐떡인다). You are thirsty. What do you need?

S: Water.

T: That's right. You need water. But how can you get water? Do you wait for the rain(고개를 들고 입을 벌린다), ah?

S: No.

T: Do you look for a water fountain and put it in your hands?

S: No. 생수를 사 먹어요.

T: You've got it. (물병을 꺼내며) Ta da. Here is a bottle of water. We need a bottle of water.

→교사는 주변에서 쉽게 볼 수 있는 용기를 준비해서 상자 안에 담아 둘 수 있다. 다양한 모양과 재질, 용도 등을 고려해서 준비하도록 한다.

74

T: We cannot hold water so we need a container. This is a plastic bottle. We can hold and carry a water bottle. Instead of a bottle, where can you put water?

S: 응답한다.

T: In a cup.

활용 어휘

- a glass, a bowl, a cup, a mug, a thermos(보온/보냉병), etc.

T: Do you like cookies?

S: Yes, I do.

T: Yes, you do, I know. Have you ever been to the store to get some cookies?

S: Yes.

T: Where were the cookies? Were they in a bottle?

S: No.

T: Were they in a paper cup?

S: No.

T: Were they in a thermos?

S: No.

T: Then where were they?

S: 과자 봉지요.

T: You are right. Cookies are in a package like this(과자 봉지를 꺼낸다). Right?

S: Right.

T: This is a package of cookies. Cookies can be put in a package. This package is made of plastic but some packages are made of paper.

T: Do you like eggs?

➤용기의 재질에 대해 설명할 때에는 용기를 직접 보여주거나 사진을 활용하여 잘 모르는 용어를 짐작할 수 있도록 한다.

➤새로운 어휘가 익숙해 질 수 있도록 한다.

75

S: Yes.

T: Where do you put eggs?

In a can? In a box? In a package? In a bottle? (용기 이름을 익힐 수 있도록 여러 가지의 용기를 언급한다.)

S: No.

T: Where do you put eggs?

S: 달걀판이요.

T: Right. We put eggs in a carton. (달걀 한 꾸러미를 꺼내며) Eggs can be put in a carton. This is an egg carton for 10 eggs. You can see egg cartons for 10 eggs, 12 eggs, 15 eggs, 20 eggs and 30 eggs. Some cartons are made of paper and others are made of plastic.

➡용기를 사용하는 목적과 이유를 묻는다.

T: Why do we put eggs in an egg carton?

S: 응답한다.

T: When we put eggs in egg cartons, we can <u>keep and carry</u> the eggs <u>safely</u> and <u>conveniently</u>. Cartons help protect eggs from damage. We should be careful not to break the eggs.

➡교사는 학생들이 자주 사용하는 용기의 그림을 그려보도록 하고 그 용기를 언제 왜 사용하는지 이야기할 수 있도록 한다.

T: Now tell me why we use containers like bottles, packages and cartons? **"When and Why do we use containers?"**

S: 왜 그리고 언제 어떤 용기를 사용하는지 자신의 경험에 비추어 친구들과 이야기를 나눈다.

T: We need containers to <u>keep food safe and fresh</u>. And the food in containers look good. When we use containers, we <u>carry food safely and conveniently</u>, too.

➡용기의 재질에 대해 설명할 때에는 용기를 직접 보여주거나 사진을 활용하여 잘 모르는 용어를 짐작할 수 있도록 한다.

T: There are many kinds of containers. <u>Containers may be made of glass, plastic, aluminum, wood, paper, etc.</u> Some containers can hold liquids and others are used to put solids. Shapes and sizes of containers are different. **"What kinds of containers do you use?"**

S: 응답한다.

- a glass, a mug, a thermos, a bottle, a box, a package, a jar, a jug, a can, a carton, etc.

T: (참치 캔을 꺼내며) This is a can of tuna. Do you like tuna? Tuna comes in a can. We can put tuna in a can. Look at this part. It is a circle. (그림을 그린다. ●-a circle) Can you tell me which one has the shape of a circle?

S: A tire. (a steering wheel, a fan, a ball, etc.)

T: Why is it a circle?

S: Because it has to roll.

T: That's right. Shapes have functions. A circle can move.

T: (우유갑을 꺼내며) This is a carton of milk. Milk comes in a carton. We can put milk in a carton. Look at this part. It is a triangle. This milk carton has two triangles. (그림을 그린다. ▲-a triangle) Which one has the shape of a triangle?

S: The top of a tower. (the top of a roof, the top of a mountain, etc.)

T: Great. A triangle usually shows the top of something.

T: This part looks like a square. It has two squares. (그림을 그린다. ■-a square) And look at this. It is a rectangle. It has four rectangles. (그림을 그린다. ▮-a rectangle) Which one has the shape of a square or a rectangle?

S: Buildings. (apartments, houses, tables, beds, refrigerators, washing machines, ovens, etc.)

T: Wow. Lots of things have the shape of a square or a rectangle. Usually they are fixed not moving. Imagine we are living in a circle house. We must be very dizzy and everything is messy.

➡Shel Silverstein의 *My Missing Piece*를 스토리텔링으로 들려줄 수 있다.

➡ ⬭ -an oval
◆ -a diamond
★ - a star
♥ - a heart
까지 학생들이 도형의 모양을 인식하고 있는지 확인해본다. 또한 이러한 도형의 모양을 가지고 있는 사물을 주변에서 찾아보도록 한다.

So shapes have functions. Well done, everyone.

T: Now design your own container. What shapes does it have?
What do you want to put there?
What are good points of your container?
Can you discuss it with your group members?

S: 모둠별로 자신들이 디자인한 용기를 보여주고 어떤 모양인지, 용도는 무엇이고 장점은 무엇인지에 대해 이야기한다.

T: 모둠별 용기 그림 중에서 가장 참신하고 실용적인 용기를 선정하여 게시한다.

Ending a Lesson

T: We talked about containers. We need containers to keep food?

S: Safe and fresh.

T: Right. To keep food safe and fresh, we need containers.
Containers have different shapes, sizes and functions. Can you tell me some shapes?

S: Circle, triangle, rectangle, diamond, star, oval and heart.

T: Those shapes are used for different functions or uses.
For example, which shape do balls and tires have?

S: They have circles.

T: Why do they have circles?

S: Because they have to move.

T: That's right. Shapes have functions.
Also containers are made of various material such as glass, plastic, aluminum, tin, paper, etc.
Look at this. This is a bottle of water. What is the bottle made of?

S: Plastic.

T: Yes. The water bottle is made of water.
Can you tell me some kinds of containers we learned?

S: A bottle of water, a can of tuna, an egg carton, a milk carton, and a package of cookies.

T: Very good.

That's all for today. Have a nice weekend and see you next time.

Bye.

B: Bye.

➤학생들이 디자인한 새로운 용기가 있으면 언급하도록 한다.

⊃ **Identify the following containers and make a dialog.**

A: What did you get at the supermarket?

B: I got _____ , _____ , _____ and _____ .

A: Did you get _____ ?

B: Oh no. I forgot _____ .

a **bottle** of water, a **container** of cheese, a **can** of beans, a **box** of cereals, a **tube** of toothpaste, a **six-pack** of soda, a **bag** of flour, a **carton** of eggs, a **plastic bag** of bread, a **roll** of paper towels, a **jar** of jam, a **package** of cookies.

a dozen eggs (*a dozen of eggs)

a loaf of bread

⊃ **Quantities**

◆ a **bunch** of _____ : flowers, bananas, grapes

◆ a **head** of lettuce

◆ a **pack** of _____ : gums, cigarettes

- a **bar** of _____ : soap, chocolate
- a **pint** of ice cream   (pint ≒ 500mℓ)
- a **quart** of milk   (quart ≒ 1000mℓ)
- a **half-gallon** of juice   (half-gallon ≒ 2ℓ)
- a **gallon** of coke   (gallon ≒ 4ℓ)
- a **liter** of sprite
- a **pound** of butter   (pound/lb. ≒ 450g)

➲ **Open your kitchen cabinets and refrigerators. Make a list of all the items you find.**

Body
What's the matter?

Goals	**Students can identify body parts and describe ailments and injuries.**
Questions	• Which parts of the body are most important at school? • How do you know that you have a cold? • What do you do when you have injuries?
Task	• Students identify each part of the body and its functions. • Students describe the symptoms of a cold. • Students talk about treatment of common injuries.
Teaching Aids	body chart, word cards, (first-aid kit)

Note

학생들이 자신의 몸 상태나 증상을 기술하기 위해서는 각 신체부위와 그 기능을 아는 것도 중요 하다. 질병이나 부상과 같은 문제가 발생했을 때 문제점을 기술하고 그에 따른 치료와 처치를 받을 수 있도록 우선 학생 자신의 신체와 그림 혹은 인형을 활용하여 각 신체부위와 기능을 익히도록 한다.

Gist of a Lesson

Starting a Lesson		
▪ Greeting ▪ Routine Questions ▪ Checking Attendance ▪ Warm-Up	▪ 교사의 신체 일부분 중 문제가 있는 곳 찾기	● 표정/동작
Developing a Lesson		
▪ Essential Question 1 ▪ Activity 1	▪ Which parts of the body are most important at school? ▪ 신체 그림을 보고 각 부분의 이름과 기능 익히기 (학생들의 사전지식에 따라 활동을 달리한다.)	● 신체 그림 ● 신체 그림 (인형 혹은 관련 동화)
▪ Essential Question 2 ▪ Activity 2	▪ How do you know that you have a cold? ▪ 교사가 표정과 동작으로 표현하는 증상 맞추기, 그 증상을 단어로 익히기	● 단어카드
▪ Essential Question 3 ▪ Activity 3	▪ What do you do when you have injuries? ▪ 평소에 개인위생을 위해 하는 일	(● 구급상자) ● 토론
Ending a Lesson		
▪ Wrap-Up	▪ 배운 내용 요약	

Teaching and Learning Plan

Starting a Lesson

T: Hello, everyone.

S: Hello, Ms. Lee.

T: How are you?

S: Not bad. And you?

T: I don't feel very well.

S: Oh.

T: What's the matter with me? Listen carefully please.

I went to see a doctor yesterday. The doctor checked my eyes and said they were okay. She checked my mouth and said it had no problem. And finally she checked this part and said it had problem.

S: Which part? (What's this part?)

T: I use this part when I hear something.

S: Ears.

T: That's right. I have some problem with my ears.

S: That's too bad.

T: Thank you for your concern. I'll be fine.

Developing a Lesson

T: Look at this body.

"Which parts of the body are most important at school?"

S: (응답한다.) e.g. My mouth is most important because I should speak and breathe.

→body chart에 있는 신체의 각 부분을 가리키며 이름과 기능을 인식하고 있는지 먼저 확인한다.

84

- My _____(body parts) is/are most important
  because I should _____(actions).
  (e.g. My hands are most important because I should write and raise.)
- Body Parts: head, face, eyes, ears, nose, mouth, teeth, tongue, chin, cheeks,
  neck, shoulders, chest, arms, elbows, hands, fingers, wrists, back, waist,
  hips, legs, knees, feet, toes
- Actions: listen to(hear), look at(see), speak(say), hold(catch), feel, taste, smell,
  breathe, chew, think, look smart/pretty/handsome, move, kick, play sports
  (basketball/volleyball/baseball/soccer, etc.), walk, sing, bend, bow, raise,
  wave, read, write, do exercise, turn, shake, swing, spin a hoolahoop, wiggle,
  support

➡ 교사는 몇 가지 예문을 만
들어 두고 어린이들의 한국어
표현을 영문으로 바꿔준다.

T: Good. Every part of the body is important and has its own
functions.

S: Sure.

T: Have you ever caught a cold? 여러분 감기 걸려본 적 있어요?
"How do you know that you have a cold?"

S: (응답한다.) I have a cough.

➡ Role Play 구문

A: You don't look
   very well.
   What's the
   matter?
B: I have____.
A: I'm sorry to
   hear that. I
   hope you get
   better soon.
B: Thank you.

활용 어휘

- I have a/an _____.
  (headache, earache, toothache, stomachache, backache, sore throat, fever,
  cough, runny nose, sore body, etc.)

T: Now let's have a role play. When I ask you the problem you
have, you can tell me some symptoms. Okay? Here we go.
Good morning, Hana. Oh, you don't look very well. What's the
matter?

S: I have a cough and a sore throat.

T: I'm sorry to hear that. I hope you get better soon.

S: Thank you.

T: What do you do when you have a cold? Tell me your own

➡ 감기에 걸렸을 때 병원에
가는 것 말고 집에서 할 수
있는 일을 경험중심으로 이야
기하도록 한다.

remedy instead of going to see a doctor.

S: (감기 걸렸을 때의 각자의 민간요법에 관해 이야기한다.)

I drink lemon/citron tea.

I sleep all day. I take a rest.

I eat a lot. I eat something hot. I eat meat. I eat porridge.

I take a bath. I take a hot bath. I take a hot shower.

T: Did it work?

S: Yes, it did.

T: You have good remedies. I'd better use them for myself.

T: Now I'll show you some symptoms. Look at my face and body carefully and tell me what is my problem.

    A: How do you feel?

    B: Not very well.

    A: What's the matter?

    B: I feel(dizzy를 답할 수 있도록 연기를 한다.)

S: 어지럽다.

T: Right. I feel dizzy. (교사는 'dizzy'라 적혀있는 카드를 보여주고 보드에 붙인다.)

T: Do you feel dizzy?

S: No.

T: What's the problem? I (cough) a lot. ('cough'가 나올 수 있도록 연기한다.)

S: 기침이요.

T: I cough a lot. ('cough'단어카드를 보여주고 보드에 붙인다.)

> **활용 어휘**

- What's the problem? I _____ a lot.
  (cough, hiccup, sneeze, vomit/throw up, bleed, burp)

→교사가 먼저 표정과 동작으로 증상과 부상을 표현하면서 어휘를 숙지시키고, 교사가 어휘를 이야기하면 학생이 동작과 표정으로 표현하고, 그 다음에는 학생들끼리 어휘를 말하고 동작을 표현할 수 있도록 한다.

→학교에서 자주 발생하는 부상에 관한 어휘를 익히도록 한다.

T: What happened? I (sprained/twisted my ankle).

S: 다리 부러지다. 발목 삐끗하다.

T: I sprained my ankle. ('sprain'을 보드에 붙인다.)

- What happened? I _____ my _____(body parts).
  (scraped, bruised, burned, hurt, cut, broke)
- I broke my leg.

T: Why don't you talk about injuries or ailments that happened to you? **"What do you do when you have injuries?"** (교사는 학생들이 숙지한 어휘를 활용하여 자신이 겪었던 부상에 관한 이야기를 서로 서로 나눌 수 있도록 한다. 아이들의 이야기를 들어보고 가장 흔하게 발생해서 모두가 주의해야할 내용이 있으면 여러 친구들 앞에서 경험을 이야기 해보도록 한다.) Jinny, can you tell us about your experience?

S: Last week I helped my mom to cook. I burned my hand.

T: What did you?

S: I put my hand in cold water and ice. And my mom applied ointment. It was not serious.

T: We should be very careful when we use fire.
When we are very very careful, we can protect ourselves against injuries.

T: Now let's talk about our treatment of injuries. When you cut your finger, what do you do?

S: 깨끗이 씻고 약을 발라요.

T: Wash the cut with water(or antiseptic cleansing wipe) and put a bandage on it. If it is serious, you should go to see a doctor. When you burn your hand, what do you do?

S: 차가운 물에 담가요.

➔부상이 있을 때 처치법에 관해 이야기한다. 아이들에게 좋은 정보가 되기 때문에 'Go to the school nurse' 혹은 'Go to see a doctor'라 하지 말고 구급함(First Aid Kit)을 가지고 와서 보여주면서 설명하는 것도 좋다.

T: Like Jinny did, we should put it in cold water and apply ointment for burns. If it is serious, you should go to see a doctor. Now you scrape your knee. It happens quite often. What are you going to do?

S: 소독하고 약 발라요.

T: You say like a doctor and a nurse. Stop the bleeding(Stanch) first, wash it and apply antibiotic ointment on it.

T: Thank you, everyone. We talked about ailments, symptoms and injuries. If anything happens at school, please let me know. What do you do for your personal hygiene? 여러분은 개인위생(신체의 청결)을 위해서 어떻게 하고 있나요?

S: I wash my hands. I take a shower. I brush my teeth. I wash my hair. I gargle. I clip my fingernails and toenails.

T: Great. We had a great time to take care of ourselves.

Ending a Lesson

T: Today we talked about body parts, symptoms of a cold and our own remedies for a cold. Also we shared our experience of common injuries and treatment of those injuries. Can you describe ailments and injuries when you have them?

Ss: Yes.

T: I hope you take good care of yourself and free from ailments and injuries.

Ss: Thank you.

T: Have a healthy day and see you again.

Ss: You, too. Thank you.

T: Bye.

Ss: Bye, Teacher.

➜ 신체부위를 익힐 때 활용하면 좋은 책

Go Away, Big Green Monster by Ed Emberley	From Head to Toe by Eric Carle	Here Are My Hands by Bill Martin Jr

➜ 신체부위를 익힐 때 활용하면 좋은 활동: 바디페인팅

학생들의 실제 몸에 페인팅을 할 수 없으므로 그룹별(2~3그룹)로 전지를 준비해서 신체의 외형만 간략하게 그리도록 한다(한 학생이 전지 위에 누우면 신체를 따라 그리는 것도 재미있다). 신체의 어느 부위에 어떤 모양과 색을 사용해서 꾸밀 것인지 조원들과 의논하여 바디페인팅을 하도록 한다. 벽이나 보드에 본을 붙여놓고 릴레이 형식으로(한 사람당 시간 제한을 두면 훨씬 더 박진감 있는 활동이 된다) 페인팅을 해도 되고 그룹별로 만족스럽게 완성한 그림을 붙여 놓고 비교해 보는 것도 좋다. 갑작스럽게 교사가 지시를 내리거나 몇 가지만을 지시할 경우에는 어린이들의 집중력과 듣기 능력을 향상시킬 수 있으나 전적으로 지시에 의존하여 수동적인 활동이 되지 않도록 한다.

⊃ **Draw the following body parts.**

head, hair, face, forehead, ear, eye, eyebrow, eyelid, eyelashes, iris, pupil, cornea, nose, nostril, cheek, cheekbone, freckles, mouth, lip, tongue, teeth, gums, chin, jaw neck, shoulder, chest, breast, abdomen, arm, elbow, hand, wrist, palm, back(of the hand), thumb, finger, knuckle, fingernail, back, waist, hip, buttocks, leg, thigh, knee, calf, shin, foot, ankle, heel, toe, toenail, sole (of the foot), top (of the foot)

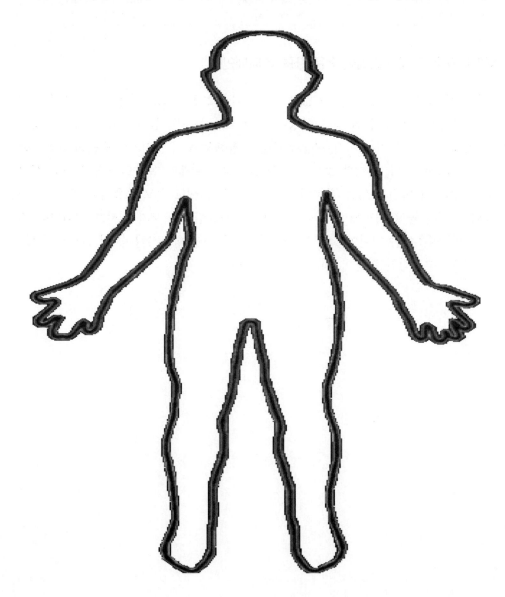

⊃ Name the following parts of the body in Korean.

esophagus	pancreas	skull
windpipe	kidneys	spine
lungs	bladder	spinal cord
heart		rib
liver	bones	ribcage
gallbladder	muscles	pelvis
stomach	veins	joint
(large/small) intestine	arteries	

식도, 기도, 폐, 심장, 간, 담낭, 위, (대/소)장, 췌장, 신장, 방광, 뼈, 근육, 정맥, 동맥, 두개골, 척추, 척수, 갈비뼈, 늑골, 흉곽, 골반, 관절

⊃ Medical Specialists

acupuncturist(침술사), allergist(알레르기 전문의), audiologist(청능사), cardiologist(심장 전문의), chiropractor(지압사), counselor/therapist(상담사), ENT(ear, nose and throat) specialist(이비인후과 전문의), gynecologist(부인과 전문의), obstetrician(산과 전문의), ophthalmologist(안과의사), orthopedist(정형외과의사), orthodontist(치열교정의사), pediatrician(소아과의사), physical therapist(물리치료사), psychiatrist(정신과의사)

⊃ Foot Reflexology

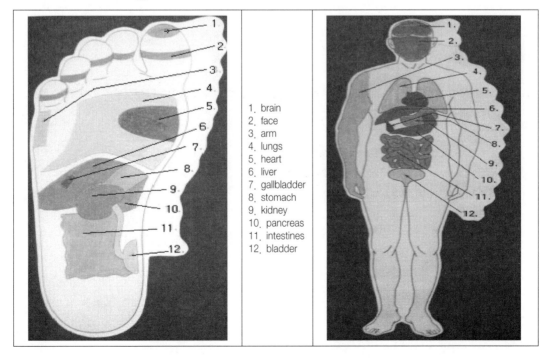

1. brain
2. face
3. arm
4. lungs
5. heart
6. liver
7. gallbladder
8. stomach
9. kidney
10. pancreas
11. intestines
12. bladder

Neighborhood
Where is the bookstore?

Goals	**Students can identify places in the neighborhood and give directions.**
Questions	• What is your favorite place in your neighborhood? What do you do there? • If you were a mayor, what place would you like to build?
Task	• Students identify places in their neighborhood and describe them. • Students talk about the places they want in their neighborhood. • Students can give directions.
Teaching Aids	Neighborhood Map, Paper(for maps and cards)

Note

장소 이름과 길안내 표현을 실생활과 관련지을 수 있도록 하고 다음과 같이 정해진 문장을 주입식으로 지도하지 않도록 한다.

Q. Where is the bus stop?

A. Go straight two blocks. Turn right at the corner.

   Go straight one block. Turn left at the corner.

   It's on your right. You can't miss it.

Gist of a Lesson

Starting a Lesson		
• Greeting • Routine Questions • Checking Attendance • Warm-Up	• 우리 동네 지도 보여주기	• 동네 지도
Developing a Lesson		
• Places in my neighborhood	• 우리 동네에 어떤 곳인지 그 곳에서 무엇을 하는지 퀴즈 형식과 직접 설명으로 지도를 가리키며 이야기한다.	• 동네 지도
• Activity 1 • Essential Question 1	• 우리 동네 지도 그리고 설명하기 • What is your favorite place in your neighborhood? What do you do there?	• 그림 종이
• Activity 2	• 시장에 된다면 우리 동네에 무엇을 짓고 싶은지 빈 카드에 적기	• 카드 종이
• Essential Question 2	• If you were a mayor, what place would you like to make?	
• Activity 3	• 지도를 보고 특정 장소로 가는 길안내를 하기	• 학생 지도
Ending a Lesson		
• Wrap-Up	• 배운 내용 요약	

Teaching and Learning Plan

T: Morning, Students.

S: Morning, Teacher.

T: How are you?

S: Very well, thank you.

T: Is it Tuesday today?

S: No. It is Thursday.

T: So you mean today is July 7th?

S: Yes, it is.

T: Wow time flies like an arrow.

(학생들을 둘러보며) No one is missing. I'm happy to see you all.

Why don't you exchange greetings in English? Remember to smile.

S: Hi. Hi, how are you? Good, thanks.

(학생들이 서로 인사를 나누는 동안 지도를 붙인다.)

T: You look much brighter now.

(지도를 가리키며) This is my neighborhood map.

There are many places in my neighborhood. Let's check them together.

Developing a Lesson

T: This is the place I visit once a week. What do I do there? I buy some bread.

S: 빵집.

T: Right. Bakery. Where is the bakery? (지도를 가리키며) Here it is.

→교사는 우리 동네에 있는 곳과 그 곳에서 하는 일을 연관시켜 지도를 설명하고 학생들이 자신이 좋아하는 장소에 대해 이야기 할 때 도움이 될 수 있도록 한다.

94

T: This is the place you study and play with teachers and friends.

S: School.

T: The school is here. (지도를 가리킨다.)

> **활용 어휘**

- There is/are _____(places) in my neighborhood.
  (e.g. There is <u>a church</u> in my neighborhood.)

- a library, a beauty salon, a neil shop, a school, a restaurant, a daycare (childcare) center, a laundromat, a dry cleaner, an apartment building, a community center, a supermarket, a park, a post office, a bank, a coffee shop, a playground, a fitness center, a clothing shop, a stationery shop, a real estate agency, a hospital, a drugstore/pharmacy, a flower shop, a gas station, a car wash, a butcher, a fast food restaurant, a crammer, a language school, a bar, an auto service center, a clinic, a dental clinic, a cosmetics shop, a massage shop, an Internet cafe, a pizza shop, a grocery store

- People _____(actions) in the _____(places).
  (e.g. People <u>read books</u> in the <u>library</u>.)

- have a haircut, get a manicure, learn something, order and eat food, take care of children, wash clothes, dry clean clothes, live and rest, get community service, buy things to eat and use, take a walk, send letters, save money, drink coffee, play on the swing/slide/see-saw/jungle gym, exercise/do physical exercise, buy clothes, buy pencils/notebooks/crayons/pens, buy and sell houses/buildings, get hospital treatment, buy (prescription or over the counter) drugs, buy flowers, fill the car, wash the car, buy meat, eat fast food, do extra study, learn a foreign language, drink beer or wine, repair cars, see a doctor, see a dentist, buy cosmetics, get a massage, use computers and play computer games, eat pizza(get pizza delivery), buy fruit and vegetables

➤학생들의 수준에 따라 수업 시간에 다룰 'places'의 개수와 어휘 수준을 고려하도록 한다.

➤학생들은 자신들이 사는 동네를 떠올리며 간략한 지도를 완성할 수 있다. 또한 지도에서 가장 특징적인 것 위주로 교사와 친구들에게 이야기할 수 있다. 교사는 표현하는데 어려움을 겪는 친구들에게 'There is/are ___ in my neighborhood' 등을 지정해서 동네를 소개할 수 있도록 한다.

T: There are lots of places to go in my neighborhood. How about you? Can you draw a map of your neighborhood?

S: Sure. (동네 지도를 그린다.)

T: Are you done? Great. Who wants to talk about the map first? Sunny, go ahead, please.

S: Yes. This is my neighborhood. There are many beauty salons and nail shops. My neighbors are very beautiful.

T: I'm sure you're right. Thank you, Sunny. Yoon, can you tell us about your map?

S: There are many pizza and chicken shops in my neighborhood. Our neighbors love pizza and chicken. But they don't eat at the shops. They eat them at home. So we can see many 배달원.

T: I see. There are many delivery delivery people in your neighborhood.

In my case, I sometimes call for pizza. It is convenient.

(교사는 학생들 모두가 돌아가며 자신들이 그린 지도에 대해 이야기할 수 있는 기회를 준다.)

> ➔교사는 학생들의 이야기를 경청하고 공통점이나 특이사항을 기억/기록해 두었다가 마무리할 때 사용한다.

T: Thank you all for talking about your maps. All of the maps have something in common. There are beauty salons, pizza and chicken shops, restaurants, Internet cafes, grocery stores, and schools. (교사는 학생들이 그린 지도의 공통점에 관해 이야기한다.)

T: **"What is your favorite place in your neighborhood? What do you do there?"** For example, my favorite place is the library. I read books, see a movie and use a computer. Why don't you talk about your favorite place with your group members?

S: (자신이 가장 좋아하는 곳이 어디이며 그 곳에서 무엇을 하는지 이야기한다. 교사는 학생들의 이이기를 듣고 개별, 모둠별 그리고 전체 대상으로 반응한다. 앞의 '지도 기술'에서 연습했으므로 학생들은 쉽게 답변할 수 있다.) e.g. My favorite place is the library. I can read books, see movies and use computers.

T: Hmm. I hear most of you choose restaurants. I don't have to ask you why.

> ➔교사는 학생들이 자신들의 동네에 무엇이 필요한지 생각해보도록 하고 사전을 찾아 영어 단어를 쓰도록 한다.

T: What would you do if you were a mayor? What would you build in your neighborhood? Think about it and write down on this card. Get one and pass them around, please. (단어가 적혀있지

않은 빈 카드를 한 장씩 나누어준다.) If you are not sure about the spellings, you can look up the dictionary. What would you do if you were a mayor? (교사는 학생들이 시장이 된다면 동네에 어떤 곳을 만들고 싶은지 카드에 적어볼 수 있도록 돕는다.)

T: Danny, if you were a mayor, what place would you build in your neighborhood?

S: I would build a movie theater.

T: Why do you want to build a movie theater?

S: My neighbors would not travel far or wait in the long line to see a movie.

T: That's a great idea. You love movies.

S: Yes, I do.

T: Thank you, Danny. Angela, **"If you were a mayor, would place would you like to build?"**

S: I would build a fire station and a police station.

T: For the safety of neighbors?

S: Yes. I hope my neighbors get help quickly when they need it.

T: Your neighbors would love you. Thank you. (교사는 학생들 모두가 발표할 수 있는 기회를 준다.)

T: Now place your card on your map. You can paste it wherever you want. Also mark where you are. (학생들은 장소 카드를 지도에 붙이고 자신이 현재 위치를 표시한다.) Now you're going to the place you pasted. You should start from the point you marked. Before you give directions, let me tell you useful expressions. ↑ (손동작) Go straight, ↱(손동작)Turn Right, ↰(손동작)Turn Left, ⇥(손동작)It's on your Right, ⇤(손동작)It's on your Left. (지도를 가리키며)These are blocks. If I go to the church from my house(한 지점에서 다른 지점으로 이동하는 예를 보여주면서), I go straight three blocks and turn left. It's on my left. (교사는 'Go straight, Turn right, Turn left' 같은 단순한 표현으로 길안내를 시작하도록 한다.)

➥길을 안내하는 표현을 가르칠 때에는 화살표와 손동작 및 몸 전체로 이동하면서 이해를 돕는다. 학생들의 수준에 따라 어휘수준을 고려한다. 길 이름을 표기할 수도 있다.

Q. Where is the _____(places)?

A. _____.

Go straight three blocks.

Go two blocks to Main Street.

Go straight three blocks and turn left on Main Street.

Go just one block and turn to the right at the corner.

Make a left turn at the corner and go straight.

It's on your right. It's on your left.

You can't miss it.

T: Sujin, come up to the front and show your map to your friends. Choose one place and ask directions, please.

S: Where is the bookstore?

S: Go straight two blocks. Turn left. Go straight one block.

S: Thank you.

(교사는 학생들이 각자가 만든 지도를 활용하여 짝 활동 및 모둠 활동으로 길안내를 할 수 있도록 한다. 기본 표현이 익숙해지면 어휘를 늘려나가도록 한다.)

Ending a Lesson

T: Was it fun to draw a neighborhood map and talk about it?

S: Yes, it was.

T: Great. There are many places in the neighborhood. I remember your favorite place is the restaurant where you eat delicious food. Right?

S: Yes. We like restaurants.

T: Still you want some more places. You said that If you were mayors, you would build movie theaters, police stations, fire stations, department stores, etc. I fully understand What you mean.

T: It's almost time to stop. Have a perfect day. Bye.

S: Bye.

⊃ **Look at the following traffic signs used in the States. Compare them with those in Korea.**

Traffic Signs

STOP	STOP	ONLY	LEFT TURN ONLY		PEDESTRIAN CROSSING
YIELD	YIELD	ONLY	RIGHT TURN ONLY	RESERVED PARKING	HANDICAPPED PARKING
DO NOT ENTER	DO NOT ENTER	ONLY	STRAIGHT THRU ONLY	PARKING	BICYCLE PARKING
	NO RIGHT TURN	SPEED LIMIT 50	SPEED LIMIT		MERGE
	NO LEFT TURN	ONE WAY	ONE WAY	DEAD END	DEAD END/ NO OUTLET
	NO U-TURN	NO PARKING ANY TIME	NO PARKING		SLIPPERY WHEN WET

⊃ **Look at the following 'Types of Vehicles' and complete a dialog.**

bicycle/bike, convertible, hatchback, hybrid, jeep, limousine, minivan, motorcycle, pickup truck, R.V.(recreational vehicle)/camper, sedan, scooter, sports car, station wagon, S.U.V.(sport utility vehicle), tow truck, tractor trailer, truck, van

A: Do you drive a/an_____?

B: No. I drive a/an _____.

A: What is your favorite type of vehicle?

B: I like _____ because ( ).

A: Which company makes the best one?

B: In my opinion, ( ) makes the best one.

➲ **What is your favorite types of vehicles?**

Do you visit your parents during traditional holidays? How do you get there? How much does it cost?

The Lazy Man

Goals	
Questions	
Task	
Teaching Aids	

Note

Gist of a Lesson

Starting a Lesson		
▪ Greeting ▪ Warm-Up		
Developing a Lesson		
▪ Activity 1 ▪ Essential Question 1 ▪ Essential Question 2 ▪ Activity 2 ▪ Essential Question 3 ▪ Essential Question 4 ▪ Activity 3		
Ending a Lesson		
▪ Wrap-Up		

Scene 1

Once there lived a man who spent the whole day doing nothing. Even during the busiest time of the farming season, he just slept and snored while the rest of his small village went to work. The villagers called him lazybones and spoke ill of him. "Get out into the fields and do some work," his mother yelled at him. He yawned and went back to sleep. His wife woke him up and said, "Please go out and help your old mother." "Don't bother me. I'm so tired of even wiggling my toe," shouted the lazy man. Then he jumped out of bed and ran off to a quiet place to sleep.

My story

The man was walking down the road without shade along the path. When he reached the ridge of a nearby mountain, he saw a hut with a straw roof. The hut was so old that it was barely standing. On the wooden floor was an old man making an ox mask. "Excuse me," The lazy man stopped to look and said to the old man, "Why are you making a mask of an ox head for? It seems to me that you have too much time on your hands. What you're doing looks worthless and useless." The old man laughed and said, "There is no such thing as worthless and useless. Also this is a present for a person who doesn't want to work." "Really? Can I try it on?" said the lazy man with amazement. "Why not? Try it on!" said the old man as he quickly place the mask on the lazy man's face. Then he cover the lazy man's back with the ox hide.

"It's very hot. Help me get this thing off!" he begged and tried to pull the mask off. The mask would not come off and the leather would not come off either. His words sounded like an ox saying, "Moo! Moo!" The lazy man ran around in circles, lowing just like an ox. "You lazy man, you are not a human being anymore. You are an ox. Come with me," said the old man. He held the leather strap and led the lazy man to the market.

My story

Scene 4

At the market, the old man said to a local farmer, "Look. Remember this. You should make sure you keep him away from the radish fields. If he eats any radish, he will die." "It sure is peculiar," said the farmer. He led the lazy man to an ox home just like an ox from the market. "I am not an ox. Please pull the head off me," cried the lazy man. But the farmer heard the ox mooing.

My story

106

Scene 5

From the next day, the lazy man had to get up early in the morning and work so hard. "Hurry up, you stupid ox! Why are you acting so lazy?" yelled the farmer as he hit the back of the lazy man with a big stick. The lazy man had to eat only hay and sleep in the dirty pen. He was so tired after working in the fields all day.

My story

It was very hot and the work was very tough. He worked and worked all day, plowing the fields and pulling a heavy wagon. When the sun set, the lazy man was led to his pen. He was very tired, but he couldn't sleep. 'I guess this is my punishment for being lazy,' he thought to himself. All he could do was cry and think about his family. "I'd rather die than be an ox" He said to himself. Suddenly he remembered what the old men said to the farmer. "That's it. I'll eat some radish," said the lazy man, making up his mind.

My story

Scene 7

The lazy man broke out of the pen and went over to the radish fields. He started to eat some radish. Just as he was doing so, the ox mask fell off his face. "What's happening?" He wondered out loud. Soon the ox leather fell off his back and he became a man again.

My story

Scene 8

"Now I'm alive. I'm a human being again," cried the lazy man and he explained the whole story to the farmer. Then he headed back to his family. Once home, he set out to work in the fields and worked hard all day. From that day on, he was known as the hardest and the most diligent man in the village.

My story

Family and People
What do you want to be?

Goals	**Students can describe their families and role models.**
Questions	• Who are the role models for you? • What do successful people have?
Task	• Students identify family members. • Students describe family members and amazing people. • Students talk about their jobs in the future.
Teaching Aids	family pictures(여러 가족의 사진), celebrity pictures(유명인 사진)

Note

다음과 같은 질문과 답변으로 가계도에 있는 가족 구성원의 지칭과 직업 이름에 국한시키지 않는다.

Q. Who is he/she?   A. He is my father/She is my mother.

Q. What does he/she do?   A. He/She is a teacher/doctor.

또한 다양한 유형의 '가족'과 가족과 이웃 안에 있는 '직업'을 이해하며 자신의 '본보기상'은 누구이며 '장래희망'은 무엇인지 생각해 볼 수 있는 장을 마련해 준다.

Gist of a Lesson

Starting a Lesson		
- Greeting - Routine Questions - Checking Attendance - Warm-Up	 - 인생에서 가장 소중한 것은 가족	
Developing a Lesson		
- Families - Activity 1 - Essential Question 1 - Activity 2 - Essential Question 2	- 여러 가족사진(5가족)을 보여주며 간단히 소개한다. 사진이 없을 경우에는 간단한 그림을 그리도록 한다. - 우리 가족 그리고 설명하기 가족사진을 미리 준비해 와서 소개할 수도 있다. - Who are the role models for you? - 본보기상(role models)의 특징을 살려 그림으로 그려보기 외모 기술하기 - What do successful people have?	● 가족사진 ● 종이 ● 유명인 사진 ● 종이
Ending a Lesson		
- Wrap-Up	- 배운 내용 요약	

Teaching and Learning Plan

Starting a Lesson

T: Hello, young ladies and gentlemen.

S: Hello.

T: How's it going?

S: Pretty good.

T: Good. Jiyoung, do you like Friday?

S: Yes, I do.

T: How about all of you? Do you like Friday?

S: Yes, I do.

T: I know. No class for tomorrow.

TGI Friday! It's September 5th. Right?

S: Yes, yes.

T: Everyone is here? (학생들을 둘러보며) Good, everyone is here to join the class.

What is the most important thing in your life? Asked this question, some people say money, some say success and some say happiness. But most people say their family is the most important. How about you? Do you agree with that?

S: Yes, I do.

Developing a Lesson

T: Families come in all different sizes and different kinds. Let me introduce some families. (여러 가족의 사진을 하나씩 보여주며)

❶This is Eunjoo's family. Eunjoo has a father, mother and a younger brother. They have a cat and a dog at home.

❷This is Tom's family. Tom lives with his mother. His dad lives

➡교사는 같은 민족의 두 부모와 자녀들이 존재하는 기존의 가족 개념을 깨고 조손(祖孫)가족, 한부모가족, 다문화가족 등 여러 유형의 가족이 있다는 것을 보여준다. (적절한 사진을 붙여서 만들 수 있다.)

113

far away. Although he sees his parents just one at a time, they both love him all the time.

❸This is Hana's family. She lives with her old grandma. Grandma is the head of her family.

❹This is Min's family. He has a father, a mother and two sisters. His mother is from Vietnam. He sometimes go to Vietnam to see his grandparents.

❺This is Jessica's family. Her father is from the United States. She is the only child. She feels lonely when she is alone at home.

T: Families have different sizes and kinds but mine is just right for me. Well, why don't you show your family? Get one and pass around these sheets of paper. Draw your family on the paper please.

S: 가족의 모습을 종이에 그린다.

T: Can you introduce your family? If you don't know how to start, you can do like this. "This is my family. This is my father. My father is a company employee. He is kind and generous. This is my mother. She is a housewife. She is a good cook. This is me. I want to be a scientist in the future." Practice with your partner first.

S: 옆 사람과 가족 소개 연습을 한다. 교사는 학생들이 힘들어하는 표현을 영문으로 바꾸어 준다.

➜학생들은 가족의 그림을 그리는 것 대신 가족사진을 준비해 올 수도 있다.

（ 활용 구문 ）

- This is my _____(family members and relatives).
  (e.g. This is my <u>sister</u>.)
- grandfather, grandmother, father, mother, brother, sister, baby, son, daughter, grandson, granddaughter, husband, wife, uncle, aunt, cousin, nephew, niece, father-in-law, mother-in-law, son-in-law, daughter-in-law, brother-in-law, sister-in-law

- My _____(family members and relatives) is a/an _____(jobs).
  (e.g. My mother is a <u>baker</u>.)

- an accountant, an actor/actress, an architect, an artist, a babysitter, a baker, a barber, a businessman/businesswoman, a butcher, a carpenter, a chef/cook, a child day-care worker, a computer software engineer, a construction worker, a customer service representative, a delivery person, an engineer, a factory worker, a farmer, a firefighter, a fisher, a gardener, a hairdresser, a homemaker, a housekeeper, a reporter, a lawyer, a mail carrier, a manager, a manicurist, a mechanic, a messenger/courier, a mover, a musician, a pharmacist, a photographer, a pilot, a police officer, a repair person, a salesperson, a sanitation worker/trash collector, a secretary, a security guard, a serviceman/servicewoman, a shopkeeper, a teacher(an instructor), a translator(an interpretor), a vet(veterinarian)

T: Now, you must be ready to introduce your family. Who can start? Any volunteers? Luna, come to the front and introduce your family.

S: (그림을 보여주며) This is my family. This is my mother. My mother is a make-up artist. This is my aunt. She is a professor. My dad is in the heaven. I am the only child but I have a puppy. His name is Roy. I want to be an anchorwoman. I love my family. Thank you.

T: Terrific. Thank you, Luna.

S: 학생들은 돌아가며 가족을 소개한다. 소개하는 학생이 듣는 학생들에게 혹은 듣는 학생이 소개하는 학생들에게 질문을 할 수도 있다.

T: When I was young, my mom was the role model for me. I wanted to be a diligent and honest person who took care of children very well. How about you? **"Who are the role models for you?"** 여러분은 닮고 싶은 본보기상이 있나요? Why do you want to follow them?

First of all look at this picture. Do you know who they are?

S: 음악가요.

T: Right. They are famous composers-Beethoven, Tchaikovsky and

→좌측의 직업은 모두 알고 있으면 좋으나, 익숙하지 않다고 해서 두려워할 필요는 없다. 학생들의 반응은 교사의 기대 이상이므로 학생들이 이야기하는 직업 중 좌측에 없는 것은 기록해 두도록 한다. 예를 들어 한 학생이 주변에 **관제사**가 있어서 그런 직업을 원한다면, **an air (traffic) controller**를 기록해둔다.

→학생들 모두가 자신의 가족을 소개할 수 있는 기회를 준다. 지원하여 발표할 수도 있고 발표한 학생이 다른 학생을 지목할 수도 있다.

Mozart.

Some people want to follow them because they want to make beautiful music like these composers.

composer

T: Now draw you role models and describe them. You can talk about their appearance and character.

S: 각자가 본받고 싶은 본보기상(role model)을 그림으로 그리고 외모나 성격적 특징을 간단하게 이야기 한다.

➡이 수업을 위해서 1~2주 전에 미리 학생들이 닮고 싶은 본보기상과 이유를 조사해서 외모와 성격 관련 표현을 영문으로 준비해 두도록 한다.

➡그림을 그리는 것에 지나치게 시간과 노력을 소모하지 않도록 한다.

ice skater

T: Are you done? Who wants to start first?

S: My role model is Kim Yuna. She is smart and works hard.

T: Do you want to be an ice skater like Yuna?

S: No, but I want to be a well-known person like her.
She helped Pyungchang host 2018 Winter Olympics.

T: I see. This lady in the picture is Sonja Henie. She was a popular skater like Kim Yuna and she became an actress.

➞학생들이 이야기하는 그들의 본보기상 특징은 성공한 사람들이 갖춘 요인이 될 수 있다.

author

S: My role model is Joan K. Rowling. She wrote *Harry Potter* Series. I love *Harry Potter* Series. She is a good writer. I want to write great books like *Harry Potte*r Series.

T: Good. I hope your dream will come true. Here are some famous authors. This one is Charles Dickens who wrote *Great Expectations* and the left bottom is Emily Bronte who wrote *Wuthering Heights*.

─────

활용 구문

- **A:** Who is your role model?
  B: My role model is _____(본보기상의 이름).
  A: Why do you want to follow him/her?
  B: _____(업적, 성격, 외모)

➞다음은 어떤 특성을 갖춘 사람에게 적합한가?
❶public employee
❷athlete
❸pastry chef
❹entertainer
❺professor

- nice(좋은), gentle(온순한), open-minded(편견이 없는), easy-going(느긋한), friendly(다정한), diligent(부지런한), generous(관대한), broad-minded(아량 있는), positive(긍정적인), active(적극적인), optimistic(낙천적인), romantic(낭만적인), humorous(유머 있는), patient(인내심 있는), polite(예의 바른), soft-hearted(상냥한), calm(침착한), witty(재치 있는), etc.

➜ 위와 같은 사람의 **성격**에 대한 질문은 'What is he/she like?'라 하고 아래의 **외모** 관련 형용사를 사용할 수 있는 질문은 'What does he/she look like?'이다.

- handsome, beautiful, cute, pretty, good-looking, tall, average height, short, fat, chubby, slender, thin, brown eyes, straight/wavy/curly/long/short hair, a beard, a mustache, sideburns, freckles, dimples, big/small eyes, etc.

T: So what do you think successful people have? **"What do successful people have?"** 성공한 사람들은 어떤 특징이 있을까요? Can you talk about it with your group members?

S: 성공한 사람들이 갖추고 있는 것에 대해 이야기 한다.

T: So you think successful people have passion, hard working, devotion, patience, challenge, dream, sacrifice, goals, etc. Which one is the most important thing for you?

S: I give up easily. So I need patience.

S: I need concentration.

S: I should have specific goals.

T: Well done, everyone. Thank you for your active participation. I hope you will be better people than your role models in the future.

➡성공한 사람들이 갖추고 있는 내적인 요건에 대해 이야기 하도록 한다.

Ending a Lesson

T: Today we talked about family and our role models. Can you introduce your family?

S: Sure.

T: Great. Can you describe their appearance and character?

S: Yes, I can.

T: Remember to be careful when you ask some questions about family.

When you meet a foreigner, you can ask 'Do you have any brothers or sisters?' instead of 'How many members are there in your family?' Do you understand me?

S: Yes, I do.

T: And we saw some famous people and talked about role models.

Who is your role model?

S: 응답한다.

T: What do successful people have?

S: Passion, Goals, Devotion.......

T: What do you have now?

S: 응답한다.

T: What do you need? What are you going to have?

S: 응답한다.

T: Okay. That's enough for today. Bye.

S: Bye.

⊃ **Answer the following questions.**

1. Who is your sister's daughter?

2. Who is your father's brother?

3. Who is your mother's sister?

4. Who is your brother's son?

5. Who is your aunt's daughter?

6. What does 'siblings' mean?

7. Who is your husband's mother?

8. Who is your wife's father?

9. Who is your husband's brother?

10. Who is your wife's sister?

11. Who is your son's wife?

12. Who is your daughter's husband?

13. Who is your son's daughter?

14. Who is your daughter's son?

15. Who is your father's father?

16. Who is your mother's mother?

17. Are you single or married?

　　Who is/was your ideal spouse(husband or wife)? Describe him/her.

Practice the following dialog and check your vocabulary.

• A: What does your husband look like? • B: He's tall and heavyset with brown eyes and brown hair.	• What does your husband look like? wife mother, father brother, sister son, daughter	• He's tall and heavyset with brown eyes and brown hair. short, average height average weight, thin blue eyes, green eyes black, gray, blonde, red hair
• A: What color is Jack's hair? B: It's black. • A: What color are Kim's eyes? B: They're blue.	• short hair, shoulder-length hair, long hair • bangs, straight hair, wavy hair, curly hair, receding hair, bald • mustache, beard, sideburns	• A: I thought you said he was the short and chubby one. • B: No, quite the opposite, he's the tall and thin-faced one.
• A: You mean the dark-skinned and wavy-haired one? • B: No, quite the opposite, his girl friend is the fair and straight-haired one.	• A: I heard his wife is very elegant and very well-dressed. • B: Yeah. But her husband is quite the opposite, he is scruffy and untidy.	• A: Mary is rather unattractive and plump, right? • B: No, that is Kelly. Mary is very good-looking and slim.
• A: I expected your teacher to be middle-aged or elderly. • B: No, she is in her twenties.	• He's tall, thin, middle-aged man. • She's a short, average-weight young woman. • She has long, straight, brown hair.	• A: What is your teacher like? • B: He is sensible and easy-going.
1. optimistic vs. pessimistic 2. extroverted vs. introverted 3. relaxed vs. tense 4. sensible, down-to-earth 5. sensitive	1. sociable 2. quarrelsome 3. cruel 4. easy-going, even-tempered 5. rude, impolite 6. honest, reliable 7. jealous	1. Monica is bossy. 2. Peter is frank. 3. I found Jack self-important. 4. Christina is broad-minded. 5. Bill is nosy. 6. Annie is pushy. 7. Sunny is original.

⊃ Confusing Vocabulary

1. homemaker(전업주부) vs. housekeeper(가정부)

2. courier(택배기사) vs. delivery person(배달원)

3. mover(이삿짐 배달원) vs. designated driver(대리운전자)

4. hairdresser(미용사), barber(이발사), manicurist(매니큐어 미용사/미조사)

5. business person(사업가) vs. business owner(자영업자)

6. waiter, waitress(식당 종업원) ➔ **server**

   policeman, policewoman(경찰관) ➔ **police officer**

   steward, stewardess(승무원) ➔ **flight attendant**

   mailman(우편배달부) ➔ **mail carrier**

   chairman(회장) ➔ **chairperson**

7. (home) health care aide (재택) 간병인

Home
Where is the key?

Goals	**Students can understand why they should keep rooms tidy.**
Questions	• Why do or should you keep your rooms tidy? • Where is the key?
Task	• Students identify rooms of a home, furniture and items. • Students ask and answer the location of items. • Students read words and know the meanings.
Teaching Aids	pictures of furniture and items, word cards, paper for drawing

Note

집의 단면도를 통한 서로 다른 공간과 그 안에 있는 가구 및 물건의 이름을 무작정 암기하고 그 물건의 위치를 전치사라는 문법 용어로 익히는 것 보다 앞의 어휘와 공간 '전치사' 개념을 연결하고 다른 상황에 활용할 수 있도록 이해시키는데 필요한 활동을 고려해 본다.

Gist of a Lesson

Starting a Lesson		
▪ Greeting ▪ Routine Questions ▪ Checking Attendance ▪ Warm-Up	▪ 잃어버린 자동차 열쇠 찾기	• 거실 그림
Developing a Lesson		
▪ Activity 1	▪ 거실에 뒤섞여 있는 가구와 물건의 이름 알기 (각각 어떤 방에 배치되어야 하는지 이야기 한다.)	• 가구/물건 그림
▪ Essential Question 1	▪ Why do you keep your rooms tidy? (방을 정리 정돈하는 이유에 대한 의견을 나눈다.)	
▪ Activity 2	▪ 단어를 읽고 의미를 파악하여 적절한 장소에 위치시 키기 (집안 가구와 물건의 이름을 익힌다.)	• 단어카드
▪ Activity 3	▪ 거실에 가구와 사물을 잘 배치시키기 (거실에 적절한 그림을 골라 거실 꾸미기 활동을 한 다.)	• 거실 그림
▪ Essential Question 2	▪ Where is the key? (전치사를 사용하여 열쇠의 위치를 말할 수 있다.)	
▪ Activity 4	▪ 거실에 감춰진 열쇠 찾기 게임 (상대방 그림 속에 감춰진 열쇠를 전치사를 활용해 찾기)	• 거실그림 (개별)
Ending a Lesson		
▪ Wrap-Up	▪ 배운 내용 요약	

Teaching and Learning Plan

Starting a Lesson

T: Hi, everyone.

S: Hi, Teacher.

T: How are you, today?

S: Fine, thank you. And you?

T: Couldn't be worse.

S: What's the matter?

T: I lost my car key.

S: I'm sorry to hear that.

T: I'm sure it is in my house. Would you help me find it?

S: Sure.

T: Then I'll show my house. Look carefully at each room of my house.

Are you ready?

S: Yes.

T: Here we go.

Developing a Lesson

T: This is my livingroom. (교사는 다음과 같은 가구와 물건이 뒤섞여 있는 지저분한 거실을 보여준다.)

S: Oh my. It's so messy.

T: I know. It must be hard to find a key here.

S: I can help you.

T: Thank you very much.

My livingroom has the following furniture and items. (교사는 가구와 물건 그림을 하나씩 제시한다.)

→ 밑그림을 그려놓고 가구와 물건은 따로 그려 코팅해 둔다. 뒷면에 자석이나 벨크로를 붙여 여러 공간에 위치시킬 수 있도록 한다.

125

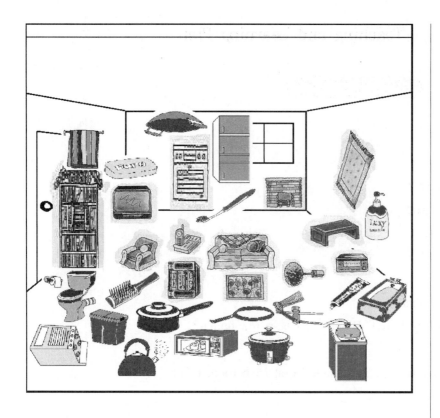

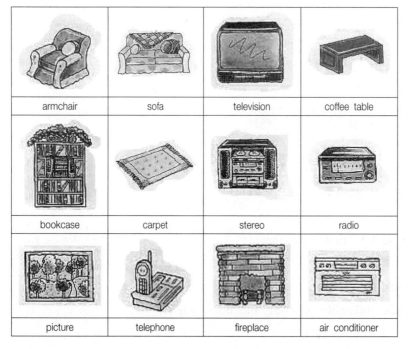

armchair	sofa	television	coffee table
bookcase	carpet	stereo	radio
picture	telephone	fireplace	air conditioner

→가정에서 볼 수 있는 가구와 물건은 그림이나 실물 등을 통해 이름을 익힐 수 있도록 한다.

126

plant	bathtub	toothbrush	toothpaste
brush	soap	towel	shampoo
toilet	shower	frying pan	saucepan
wok	microwave oven	rice cooker	refrigerator
washing machine	stove	kettle	trash can

✔ 좌측 자료의 두 번째 그림은 2인용 의자로 보이고, 2인용 의자는 'love seat'이라 한다. 3인용 이상 의자를 'sofa'나 'couch'라 하는데 여기서는 'sofa'라 칭한다.

T: My house has a livingroom, a bedroom, a kitchen and a bathroom.

The first picture is an armchair. Where should it go?

S: It should go to the livingroom.

T: Are you sure?

S: Yes, I am.

T: (주전자를 가리키며)What is this? It is a kettle. Where should it go?

S: It should go to the kitchen.

(위 그림 속 가구와 물건의 이름 및 배치되면 좋은 장소를 이야기 한다.)

T: Why do or should you keep your room tidy? Discuss it with your group members.

S: 학생들은 모둠별로 정리정돈을 하거나 해야 하는 이유에 관해 서로의 의견을 나눈다.

T: 모둠을 돌면서 학생들의 주요 아이디어를 영어로 바꾸어 준다.

활용 구문

When I keep my room tidy,
- I feel good in the clean and well-arranged room.
- I feel safe and confident with sudden visitors.
- I can find the items I need easily and quickly.
- I can save time and money.

T: I'll write rooms of my house on the board-a livingroom, a kitchen, a bedroom and a bathroom. I'll give you word cards. Get three cards and pass them on. Read the words you have and put them in proper rooms.

S: 학생들은 집안 가구와 물건에 해당하는 단어카드를 읽고 거실, 침실, 부엌과 욕실 중 해당되는 곳에 붙인다.

T: Now, arrange proper furniture and items in the livingroom.

➛의견 나누기

➛교사가 말하는 방을 듣고 그 곳에 어울리는 가구와 물건을 붙이는 활동을 할 수도 있다.

➛여러 가구와 물건이 섞여있던 거실 그림에서 가구와 물건을 떼어내어 좌측의 텅 빈 거실에 위치시킨다.

S: 학생들은 보드에 붙어 있는 단어를 한번 더 확인하고 거실에 놓으면 좋을 그림을 골라 적절한 곳에 배치한다.

➡전치사 이해하기

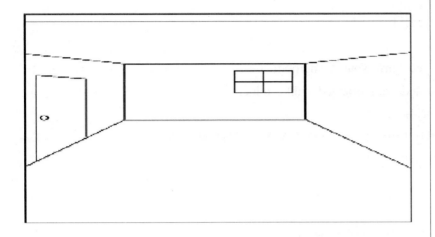

T: Now I found the key. Can you follow my directions?

S: Yes.

T: Listen carefully and look at my gestures.

The key is next to(손동작) the bookcase.

It is on the coffee table.

It is between the stereo and the radio.

It is behind the telephone.

It is under the plant.

> ### 짚고 넘어가기

- 전치사(preposition)라는 용어 보다는 장소를 가리킬 때 사용하는 표현으로 다음과 같은 것이 있다고 지도한다. 동작과 교실에 있는 사물을 활용하여 설명하고 우리말로 뜻을 이야기 하여 이해를 확인한다.
- on(위에), in(안에), under(아래에), at(지점에), behind(뒤에), in front of(앞에), beside/next to(옆에), near(가까이에), between A and B(A와 B사이에)

T: You found it. Well done.

These are useful to express locations. Can you tell me '책장 뒤에' in English?

➡숨바꼭질, 보물지도 따라가기, 장면 그림 암기해서 위치 말하기 등 여러 가지 활동으로 전치사를 익힐 수 있다.

S: Behind the bookcase.

T: 교사는 장소 전치사 몇 가지를 위와 같은 방식으로 더 확인하도록 한다.

S: 교사의 질문에 답변한다.

T: Well, why don't you draw your livingroom?

I hope it is clean and well-arranged unlike mine.

S: 학생들은 거실 그림을 그린다.

실제적으로 생활하는 것이 아닌 본인이 꿈꾸고 이상적으로 생각하는 거실을 그릴 수도 있다.

T: Are you done?

S: Yes.

T: Good. Now hide the key in your picture.

Now you should find your partner's key.

So, you have to ask questions like "Is it between the bookcase and fireplace?"

S: Can I see my partner's picture?

T: Sure. The picture of your livingroom is different from that of your partner's. To find the key, you should use expressions we learned today.

S: Can I draw the key invisible?

T: Absolutely. But it must stay at the same place. Do not make it move.

S: 학생들은 짝과 함께 전치사를 사용하여 질문하고 답하면서 상대방의 열쇠를 찾는다.

T: Who got the partner's key first? Raise your hands.

S: 먼저 상대방의 열쇠를 찾은 학생들이 손을 든다.

T: Excellent. Among the winners, anyone can come up to the front, show the picture and describe the livingroom. Brave winners? Volunteers?

S: 학생들은 자신이 그린 거실 그림을 전치사를 사용하여 묘사할 수 있다.

T: I'm sure everyone can be good artists.

Your livingroom is much better than mine.

Not only comfortable and convenient furniture but also cutting-edge items are well arranged in your livingroom.

You are so creative, aren't you?

S: Drawing a livingroom was fun.

T: I'm so happy to hear you had some fun.

S: Finding a key was fun too.

T: Great.

S: There were a lot of items and furniture in the picture.

T: When you go back home, you will find more furniture and items.

Can you draw your own bedroom?

S: Is it homework?

T: Yes. It is your homework.

Practice describing the bedroom in English. Okay?

S: Okay.

T: That's enough for today. See you next time.

S: Bye, Teacher.

To Better Teachers

⊃ **Answer the following questions.**

1. Why is a detergent better than soap for washing a frying pan?

2. What are the similarities and the differences between a pot and a saucepan?

3. Where are dishes put once they are washed and dried?

4. Who makes the meals in your home? Who washes the dishes?

5. When is a vacuum cleaner used? When is a scrubbing brush used?

6. Which of housework tasks makes you most tired-cooking, cleaning, ironing, or washing?

7. What housework have you done today? If none, why not?

8. When you make the bed, what goes between the mattress and the blanket?

9. Why should a husband help (not help) his wife with the housework?

10. You do not have a servant and you are tired. The dishes have not been washed(the automatic dishwasher is not working). The rugs are dirty and the vacuum cleaner is broken, the beds have not been made, and the children are going to be home all day. What do you do?

⊃ **Ask and answer a little faster using the following patterns.**

1. **Q:** What can you see in the livingroom? **A:** I can see _____.

2. **Q:** How do you say _____ in English? **A:** It is _____.

3. **Q:** Where is _____? **A:** It's in the _____.

* 거실: couch(sofa), armchair, love seat, rocking chair, stool, entertainment center, coffee table
* 방: dresser, closet, nightstand, pillow, pillowcase, quilt, blanket, bunk beds, safety rail
* 욕실: bathtub, faucet, grab bar, soap dish, towel rack, toilet paper, toilet seat, shower head, wastebasket, sink, drain
* 주방: paper towels, dish rack, cabinet, refrigerator, freezer, blender, microwave, pot, counter, cutting board

⊃ **Do the following instructions.**

* Describe your livingroom, bedroom, bathroom and kitchen.

* Which do you prefer to live in, a house or an apartment house? Why?

* What do you do when you have household problems?

⊃ Translate Korean into English and fill in the blank.

1. **A:** The (초인종) must be out of order.

   B: I had to check a person through a (방문자 확인용 구멍).

2. **A:** 자물쇠가 고장 났어.

   B: 그럼 자물쇠수리공을 불러.

3. **A:** The power is out.

   B: Call the ( ).

4. **A:** 수도꼭지에서 물이 새고 있어. 세면대의 물이 넘치고 변기는 막혀있지. What should I do?

   B: Call the ( ) right now.

5. **A:** 조리대 위에 바퀴벌레가 있다.

   B: 해충구제업자를 불러야겠군.

⟨Answers⟩

1. doorbell, peephole 2. The lock was broken. Why don't you call the locksmith? 3. electrician 4. The faucet is dripping. The sink is overflowing and The toilet is stopped up. plumber 5. There is a cockroach on the counter. I should call the exterminator.

Food
What is your favorite food?

Goals	**Students can describe how to make their favorite food.**
Questions	• What food is good for breakfast? Why do you think so? • What is your favorite food? What are ingredients? • How can you make your favorite food?
Task	• Students talk about good foods for breakfast. • Students identify foods and food ingredients. • Students describe how to make they favorite food.
Teaching Aids	food pictures, word cards, colored paper

Note

'음식'이란 주제가 나오면 "What's your favorite food?"라는 질문과 간단한 답변으로 끝나지 않고 음식을 다양한 각도에서 생각해 볼 수 있는 기회를 만든다. 5가지 기초 식품군, 식탁에 밥이 올라올 때까지의 과정, 여러 나라의 음식, 계절/명절/절기 음식, 한국의 대표 음식 등도 하위 주제가 될 수 있다.

Gist of a Lesson

Starting a Lesson		
• Greeting • Routine Questions • Checking Attendance • Warm-Up	 • 오늘 아침 식사로 먹은 음식 이야기하기	
Developing a Lesson		
• Essential Question 1 • Activity 1 • Activity 2 • Essential Question 2 • Activity 3 • Essential Question 3	• What food is good for breakfast? 　Why do you think so? • 사진보면서 음식 이름 익히기 　('Do you like~?' 표현을 활용한다.) • 단어 모으기 게임: 음식 재료 이름 익히기 　(보드에 붙여 놓은 단어 중 교사가 읽는 것을 찾아 　낸다.) • What is your favorite food? 　What are the ingredients of your favorite food? • 색종이로 가장 좋아하는 음식의 재료 만들기 　(재료의 모양과 색상에 맞게 색종이를 활용한다.) • How can you make your favorite food? 　(가장 좋아하는 음식의 조리법을 설명한다.)	● 음식 사진 ● 음식 사진 ● 단어 카드 ● 색종이
Ending a Lesson		
• Wrap-Up	• 배운 내용 요약	

Teaching and Learning Plan

T: Hello, how are you?

S: Very well. And you?

T: Not very well. I'm hungry.

This morning I got up late. I had no time to eat breakfast.

How about you? Did you eat breakfast?

S: Yes, I did.

T: Good. What did you eat?

S: 답변한다.

T: Good. **"What food is good for breakfast? And why do you think so?"**

Work in groups, please.

S: 학생들은 짝을 짓거나 모둠을 만들어 아침식사로 좋은 음식과 그 이유에 대해 이야기를 나눈다. 모둠별로 대표 음식을 선정해서 발표하도록 한다.

활용 어휘

- easy and simple breakfast: cereal, bread/toast/sandwiches, juice/milk, eggs, salad, *tteok*
- typical Korean breakfast: rice, soup/stew, *kimchi*, several side dishes

Developing a Lesson

T: Now Group A, tell us good food for breakfast, please.

S: We think the typical Korean breakfast is good. Usually we eat rice, soup or stew, *kimchi*, and some side dishes. We are growing, so we need energy from balanced meals. When we are hungry in the morning, we cannot enjoy studying and playing at school.

| typical Korean Breakfast | Easy and Simple Breakfast |

→교사는 학생들이 음식이름과 음식을 쉽게 연결시킬 수 있도록 사진자료를 제시하고 학생들이 더욱 다양한 의견을 낼 수 있도록 영어로만 발표하도록 강요하지 않는다.

S: I agree with Group A. It is good to eat a delicious and balanced meal in the morning. But who cooks? Mom cooks and goes to work. Haven't you had a war-like morning before? Everybody is busy and I feel sorry for mom. So we prefer easy and simple breakfast such as cereal, bread, eggs, sandwiches, toast, fruit and vegetables, milk/juice, salad, *tteok*, etc.

T: Thank you for your suggestions for breakfast meals.
Now look at these pictures.

tacos ratatouille sushi sashimi spaghetti
hamburger sandwich steak fish&chips French toast

T: Do you like steak?

S: Yes, I do.

T: Do you like sushi and sashimi?
You can eat these dishes at Japanese restaurants.

S: No, I don't.

T: Do you like spaghetti?

S: Yes, I do.

→교사가 음식에 대한 질문을 할 때에는 먼저 사진 자료를 준비하여 학생들이 사진과 단어를 연결할 수 있도록 한다. 생소한 음식일수록 사진 자료는 필수적이다.

T: As you know well, it is an Italian dish with spaghetti, ground beef, tomatoes and onions. There are many kinds of spaghetti with different ingredients.

S: 학생들은 자신들이 먹어본/알고 있는 스파게티 이름에 대해 이야기 한다.

T: Do you like tacos?

S: What is tacos?

T: It is a Mexican dish with peppers, ground beef, onions and cheese.

S: 타코스가 멕시코 스타일의 샌드위치임을 이해할 수 있다.

T: Do you like ratatouille?

S: It is a movie.

T: Right. You may remember the mouse made ratatouille. It is a French dish with eggplant, zucchini, tomatoes and onions.

S: I don't think I'll like it.

T: Do you like hamburgers?

S: Yes, I do.

T: Do hamburgers have ham inside?

S: No. It does not have any ham in it.

T: Then Why hamburgers? This food comes from Hamburg, Germany. It was easy to make, so it came to the United States with many Germans in the 19th century.

S: 교사가 준비해온 사진을 보여주며 질문하는 것을 잘 듣고 답한다.

T: Now let's play a game. I'll divide you into two groups. You are Group A and you are Group B. Stand up and make two lines, please. (아이들이 줄을 서는 동안 교사는 단어 카드를 보드에 붙인다.) Look at the board. There are some words about food ingredients. Let's read the words together. (교사는 단어를 빠른 속도로 읽어준다.) When I read a word, you come to the board,

➡ 단어카드 모으기 게임(듣기훈련 및 집중력과 순발력 요구): 두 그룹의 학생들이 각각 한 줄로 서서 한사람씩 교사가 외치는 단어를 재빨리 고른다. 단어를 고르는 시간을 제한할 수 있으며 단어 카드를 많이 가지고 있는 팀이 이긴다.

get the word and go to the back of the line. A group that has more cards wins the game. Have you got it?

S: Yes.

(ground beef) (zucchini) (tomato) (onion) (garlic)
(pepper) (eggplant) (carrot) (pork) (cucumber)
(potato) (tofu) (red pepper) (soy sauce) (soybean paste)
(red pepper paste) (red pepper powder)

T: Good. Here we go. (교사는 영어 단어를 읽는다. 한국어 의미를 이야기할 수도 있다.)

T: (게임이 끝난 후) Let's count the cards. Group A has 9 cards and Group B has 7 cards. A group wins. Congratulations!

S: 학생들은 잘 모르는 단어를 "What does 'soy sauce' mean in Korean?"과 같은 표현을 사용해서 질문하고 교사는 한국어로 답해준다.

T: **"What is your favorite food?"**

S: 응답한다.

T: **"What are the ingredients of your favorite food?"**

In my case, I like pork cutlet. My favorite food is pork cutlet. To make it, I need pork, salt, flour, eggs and oil.

(**활용 구문**)

→색종이로 음식 재료 만들기

- My favorite food is _____.
  To make it I need _____.

S: 학생들은 '아침식사에 좋은 음식'에서 익힌 음식 이름과 '단어카드 모으기 게임'에서 익혔던 재료이름을 활용하여 각자가 좋아하는 음식과 재료를 이야기하고 색종이를 사용하여 음식의 재료를 만든다.

T: (만들기가 끝나고 나서) Who wants to talk about favorite food? Show your ingredients, please. Any volunteers?

S: My favorite food is *tteokbokki*.
To make it, I need *tteok*, 어묵(fish cake) and red pepper paste.

T: White *tteok*, yellow fish cake and red *gochujang*. Wee done.

→음식 재료를 손질하는 것에 부터 조리방법에 이르기까지 의 조리법을 짝과 함께 상의하 도록 한다.

S: My favorite food is *ramyun*.
To make it, I need water, *ramyun*, 파(a green onion), and an egg.

T: Yellow *ramyun*, a green&white green onion, and a yellow&white egg. Good job.

S: I like *bibimbap*. My favorite food is *bibimbap*.
To make it, I need rice, some vegetables, 참기름(sesame oil) and *gochujang*.

T: Well, you made and talked about the ingredients of your favorite food. Now why don't you talk about the recipe with your partners? Try to find easy instructions to make your favorite food.

활용 표현

- add(첨가하다), barbecue/grill(굽다), bake(오븐에 굽다), boil(삶다), broil(그릴에 굽다), beat(치대다), break(깨다), chop(잘게 썰다), core(속/심을 도려내다), cube(깍둑썰기하다), cut(썰다), deseed(씨를 빼다), fry(튀기다/볶다), grate(갈다), microwave(전자레인지에서 돌리다), mince(다지다), mix(섞다), peel(벗기다), pour(붓다), put(놓다/놓다), roast(고기를 덩어리째 굽다), saute(부치다), simmer(약한 불에서 끓이다), slice(얇게 썰다, 한 조각 잘라내다), steam(찌다), stir(젓다), stir-fry(저으며 볶다), trim(다듬다)

T: Are you done? Let me tell you my recipe first.
My favorite food is pork cutlet. To make it, I need pork, flour and, salt, eggs and oil. Here are directions. First, Beat eggs in

a bowl and add salt. Second, coat the pork with flour. Third, coat the pork with eggs and fry it. What is this recipe for?

S: It's for pork cutlet.

T: I'll tell you another example.

My favorite food is French toast. To make it, I need milk, eggs, flour, bread and oil. Here are directions. First, Put eggs, milk, and flour in a bowl and mix them well. Second, soak the bread in the mixture. Third, heat the oil in a frying pan, and cook the bread until golden. What is this recipe for?

S: It's for French toast.

T: How can we make *tteokbokki*?

S: First, put water and red pepper paste in a pot. Second boil it stirring well. Third, add *tteok* and fish cake. Fourth, cook it until soft.

T: How about bibimbap? What is the recipe?

S: It is simple and easy. We just put rice and vegetables in a bowl, and then add sesame oil and *gochujang*.

T: (교사는 학생들이 다양한 조리법을 이해하고 말할 수 있도록 돕는다.)

It sounds like all of you are chefs now. But you have to remember this. When you cook you usually use fire and knife. It means...

S: We should be careful.

T: That's right. You should be very careful not to have a cut or a burn.

T: Now do you feel confident of cooking?

S: Yes, I do.

T: We talked about good foods for breakfast and learned some words about dishes and ingredients. What is '가지' in English?

S: It is an eggplant.

T: Which food is popular all over the world? It's from Germany, actually.

S: A hamburger.

T: Excellent. I hope you cook your favorite food with your parents. Have a good day!

S: Bye.

To Better Teachers

○ 다음은 CNN Go 편집진이 선정한(2011년 9월) '세상에서 가장 맛있는 50가지 음식들(World's 50 most delicious foods)'이다.

Which food have you tried? Do you know the recipe? How many Korean foods can you see? Can you tell foreigners the recipes of those foods?

순위	음식과 나라	순위	음식과 나라
1	Rendang, Indonesia	26	Penang assam laksa, Malaysia
2	Nasi goreng, Indonesia	27	Tacos, Mexico
3	Sushi, Japan	28	Barbecue pork, Hong Kong
4	Tom yam goong, Thailand	29	Chili crab, Singapore
5	Pad thai, Thailand	30	Cheeseburger, United States
6	Som tam(Papaya salad), Thailand	31	Fried chicken, United States
7	Dim sum, Hong Kong	32	Lobster, Global
8	Ramen, Japan	33	Seafood paella, Spain
9	Peking duck, China	34	Shrimp dumpling, Hong Kong
10	Massaman curry, Thailand	35	Neapolitan pizza, Italy
11	Lasagna, Italy	36	Moo nam tok, Thailand
12	Kimchi, Korea	37	Potato chips, United States
13	Chicken rice, Singapore	38	Warm brownie and vanilla ice cream, Global
14	Satay, Indonesia	39	Masala dosa, India
15	Ice cream, United States	40	Bibimbap, Korea
16	Kebab, Turkey	41	Galbi, Korea
17	Gelato, Italy	42	Hamburger, Germany
18	Croissant, France	43	Fajitas, Mexico
19	Green curry, Thailand	44	Laksa, Singapore
20	Pho, Vietnam	45	Roti prata, Singapore
21	Fish 'n' chips, England	46	Maple syrup, Canada
22	Egg tart, Hong Kong	47	Fettucini alfredo, Italy
23	Bulgogi, Korea	48	Parma ham, Italy
24	Fried rice, Thailand	49	Lechon, Philippines
25	Chocolate, Mexico	50	Goi cuon, Vietnam

● 우리말의 뜻에 맞는 영어 단어를 쓰시오.

맛과 식감		요리 기구	
달콤하다		냄비	
짭짤하다		도마	
쓰다		주걱	
시다		과자 모양 틀	
맵다, 매콤하다		믹서	
톡 쏘다, 얼얼하다		석쇠	
떫다		체	
담백하다		꼬챙이, 꼬치	
바삭바삭하다		거품기	
쫄깃쫄깃하다, 질기다		밀대	
말랑말랑하다		집게	
끈적거리다		솔	
딱딱하다		국자	
즙이 풍부하다		강판	
		껍질 벗기는 기구	
		뒤집는 주걱	

〈Answers〉

◆ 맛과 식감: sweet, salty, bitter, sour, hot/spicy, pungent, rough, bland/mild, crispy/crunch, chewy, soft, sticky, hard, juicy

◆ 요리 기구: pot, cutting board, spatula, cookie cutters, blender, grill, strainer, skewers, whisk, rolling pin, tongs, brush, ladle, grater, peeler, turner

⊃ Let's make Crispy French Toast together.

Ingredients	Recipe
1/2 cup fat-free milk 2 eggs or 1/2 cup egg substitute 1/4 cup orange juice 1 tbsp. flour 1 tsp. vanilla extract 11/2 cups cornflakes 6 slices bread 2 tbsp. olive oil	1. Combine eggs(or egg substitute), milk, orange juice and flour in a bowl and mix them well using a whisk. 2. Add vanilla extract to the mixture. 3. Put cornflakes in the plastic bag and crush them using a rolling pin. 4. Add bread and soak it in the mixture turning once. 5. Coat both sides of each slice of bread with cornflake crumbs. 6. Heat the oil in a frying pan, and cook the bread until golden.

Hobbies
What do you do in your free time?

Goals	**Students can describe their favorite leisure activities.**
Questions	• What do you do or want to do in your free time? • What are good leisure activities for students? • What is your favorite place to go?
Task	• Students identify common hobbies. • Students describe favorite leisure activities. • Students ask for and offer a suggestion for places to go.
Teaching Aids	pictures of hobbies, paper for activity plan

Note

'여가 활동'이 그동안 영어 시간에 다루었던 학습용 '취미'에 국한되지 않도록 학생들의 경험과 생각 등을 반영하고 '여가활동'은 왜 중요한지 앞으로 어떤 활동을 하는 것이 좋은지 의견과 정보를 나눌 수 있는 시간이 되도록 한다.

Gist of a Lesson

Starting a Lesson		
▪ Greeting ▪ Routine Questions ▪ Checking Attendance ▪ Warm-Up	▪ 수업 후에 어떤 일을 하는지 묻는다.	

Developing a Lesson		
▪ Essential Question 1 ▪ Activity 1 ▪ Activity 2 ▪ Essential Question 2 ▪ Activity 3 ▪ Essential Question 3	▪ What do you do or want to do in your free time? 　(여가 시간에 하고 있거나 하고 싶은 활동 말하기) ▪ 그림보고 여가시간에 하는 일 이야기하기 　(적절한 동사를 사용해서 그림을 기술한다.) ▪ 취미 빙고 게임 　(빙고 게임을 하면서 다양한 여가 활동 표현을 익힌다.) ▪ What are good leisure activities for students? 　(학생들에게 유익한 여가활동은 무엇인지 의견을 나눈다.) ▪ 여가 활동 계획표 만들기 　(여가 활동 계획표를 만들어 본다.) ▪ What is your favorite place to go? 　(가볼 만한 곳을 묻거나 제안할 수 있다.)	● 동작 그림 ● 빙고 그림 ● 빈종이

Ending a Lesson		
▪ Wrap-Up	▪ 배운 내용 요약	

Teaching and Learning Plan

Starting a Lesson

T: Morning.

S: Good morning.

T: How are you today?

S: Not bad.

T: Isn't it cooler and cooler day by day?

S: Yes. It is cold in the morning and it is hot in the afternoon.

T: Yes it is. The daily temperature is fluctuating(손동작) a lot recently.

Is Monday today?

S: No, it's Tuesday, October 16th.

T: Thank you. Is everybody present?

S: No. Kate is not here.

T: Oh, I got a phone call from her mother. She had a bad cold. She practiced singing and dancing a lot for TV audition program.

S: That's too bad.

T: Is there anyone who practices something after class?

S: No. I don't know.

T: What do you do after class?

S: 아이들은 수업을 마치고 어떤 일을 하는지 이야기 한다.

Developing a Lesson

T: I am sorry to hear that most of you are so busy studying and studying.

It sounds silly to ask you "What do you do in your free time?"

So I would like to change the question.

"What do you want to do in your free time?"

Could you talk about it with your group members?

S: 학생들은 여가 시간에 어떤 활동을 하고 싶은지 또는 어떤 활동을 하는지에 관해 서로 이야기 한다.

활용 구문 및 어휘

➜우리 아이들은 예전에 비해 생활환경이 나아졌음에도 불구하고 자신만의 여가 시간이 없기 때문에 먼저 흔한 취미활동 관련 그림을 보여주도록 한다.

A: What do you (want to) do in your free time?

B: I (want to) _____.

- I (want to) collect marbles(구슬)/ttakjis(딱지)/stickers(스티커)/figures(피규어)/coins(동전)/photos of celebrities(유명인 사진)/autographs of celebrities(유명인 사인), etc.
- I (want to) read books(comic books/poems/novels/fairy tales/essays, etc.)
➜ I (want to) read magazines or articles about automobiles(자동차)/fashion(패션)/movies(영화)/musicals&plays(뮤지컬&연극)/TV programs/animals/plants(식물)/architecture(건축물)/events&festivals(행사&축제)/travel(여행)/crafts(공예)/games(게임)/sports(스포츠)/culture(문화)/psychology(심리)/cooking(요리)/knitting(뜨개질)/fishing(낚시)/sewing(바느질)/dolls(인형)/music(음악) etc.
- I (want to) play soccer/baseball/volleyball/basketball/table tennis/tennis/badminton/hockey/ice hockey/football/golf/cricket, etc.
➜ I (want to) go jogging/walking/running/biking/bowling(볼링)/swimming/skating/figure skating/sledding/skiing/snowboarding/inline skating/surfing/snorkeling/scuba diving/hiking/camping, etc.
- I (want to) do Taegwondo/exercise/sing/dance/keep a pet/draw&paint pictures/cook/play musical instruments(piano, cello, flute, ocarina, guitar, drums, clarinet, oboe, etc.)/design clothes/search the Internet/take a nap/go shopping/clean the house/watch TV/go to see a movie(opera, musical, play, etc.)/write a novel/travel/watch birds/take pictures, etc.

T: Okay. look at the picture. And tell me what they do in their free time.

➜학생들이 동사를 사용하여 그림을 기술할 수 있는지 확인한다.

T: What does Jack do in his free time?

S: He cooks.

T: What does a baby do in his spare time?

S: He sleeps.

T: What do Sue and Mary do in their spare time?

S: They chatter/talk.

T: What does Mr. Sullivan do in his free time?

S: He reads a newspaper.

T: What do Charlie and Larry do in their free time?

S: They play a game.

T: What does Mrs. Smith do in her free time?

S: She watches TV.

T: Good. Let's see what other children do in their free time.

S: Okay.

T: Do you know Bingo game?

S: Yes.

T: Work in pairs. Each team has one piece of paper. (교사는 게임 자료를 나누어주고 빙고게임을 한다.)

➙게임을 활용해서 취미활동과 동작에 관한 표현을 흥미롭게 익힐 수 있도록 한다.

(그림에 나오는 어휘)

study, do a puzzle, write a letter, play a game, make a model plane, collect stamps, do a magic trick, color, sew, listen to music, take a nap, play cards, read a book, talk on the phone, play video games, use the computer, play the piano, watch TV, dance, play ping pong, take a bath, snap fingers, wiggle toes, comb hair, stretch

- What do you do in your free time?

  I _____.

- What is your hobby?

  I like _____ ~ing.

➙학생들이 두 가지 표현을 활용해서 질문과 응답을 할 수 있도록 한다.

T: Did you enjoy the game?

S: Yes.

T: You saw leisure activities to do through the game.

"What are good leisure activities for students?"

Work in groups. Talk about activities you like and choose the best one.

S: 학생들은 모둠별로 모여 그들에게 가장 좋은 여가 활동이 무엇인지 상의하고 그 중 한 가지를 고른다.

T: Okay. I'm expected to hear the best activities you chose. Whose group wants to talk first?

GA: We found there is difference between the activities we want and the good and useful activities for us.

➤교사와 부모의 시각이 아닌 학생들의 시각에서 좋은 여가 활동에 귀를 기울이도록 한다.

We love video games. We really want to play video games in our free time. But those games are just fun. They don't bring us creativity or patience. Sometimes they keep us from studying subjects or reading books. So we reached an agreement that the best leisure activity is doing origami. We just need origami paper and enjoy origami wherever we go. We can have patience, creativity and confidence through origami.

T: Thank you Group A. It is interesting to find the gap between leisure activities. Any groups?

GB: We do not agree with Group A. We make the gap. It depends on us. We think the best leisure activity is playing video games. Honestly we have no time to enjoy games during weekdays. When we do our best in our daily routines, we are deserved to enjoy video games during a weekend. In my case, I play video games for two hours every Saturday. Some students(who have good skills) like origami, but others (who are poor at using hands) don't like it. Even though the activity is good for patience and creativity, it can be stressful and the hard job.

T: Video games are best in case we control ourselves.

GC: We chose outdoor activities such as camping, hiking and picnics are good for students. Most students stay indoors. They need fresh air, trees, flowers, and so on.

➦일월, 주별, 월별, 방학 등 여가 활동 계획표를 작성하도록 한다.

T: Thank, everyone. Then tell me when you enjoy those activities you say. During the weekend? Or during summer or winter vacation? Each group has one sheet of paper and make a plan.

S: 학생들은 자신들이 선택한 여가 활동 계획표를 작성하고 교사는 이를 적절한 곳에 게시한다.

T: I am so impressed with your ideas.
Let me ask you one more question.

"What is your favorite place to go?"

Can you recommend good places?

S: 학생들은 '가볼만한 곳'에 관해 이야기한다.

→미래 시제에 사용되는 'will'
과 'be going to'가 들어 있는
대화를 완성하도록 한다.

(활용 구문)

- My favorite place is the _____, because I like _____.
- **A:** Can you recommend a good place to go?
  B: Do you like_____?
  A: Yes, I do.
  B: Then how about going to the_____?
- **A:** Do you have any plans for this weekend?
  B: No, I don't. What are you going to do?
  A: I like _____. I'll go to the _____.
  B: Have a good time.
- paintings—art gallery museum, animals—zoo, live music—concert, history—history museum, hand-made jewelry—a craft fair, flowers & trees—botanical garden, the moon & the stars—planetarium(천체투영관), sea creatures—aquarium, rides—amusement park, ballet—(ballet) theater

T: Hobbies and leisure activities can refresh our daily routines. You say you are very busy studying and no time to enjoy hobbies or leisure activities, but I hope you find good activities for you.

(Ending a Lesson)

T: We talked about what we do or want to do in our free time. Through the Bingo game, we learned new vocabulary about hobbies.

Now can you tell me what do you want to do in your free time?

S: Yes, I can.

T: Also we discussed good activities for students and made plans. What are good activities for you?

S: (각자 대답한다.)

T: Do you have any plans for a holiday?

S: Yes, I do.

T: Can you tell me the plans?

S: (각자 대답한다.)

T: Have a great holiday and see you again.

S: Bye.

To Better Teachers

○ **Complete the following dialog using different words.**

A: What do you want to do in your spare time?

B: I have no idea. Do you have any suggestions?

A: How about <u>going jogging</u>?

B: Hmm. I don't feel like <u>going jogging</u>. Any other ideas?

A: Well, how about <u>seeing a movie</u>?

B: Good idea! We haven't <u>seen a movie</u> in a long time.

1) go to the ball game, drive to the mountains

2) play tennis, ride bikes

3) go fishing, go swimming at the pool

4) have a picnic, go to the amusement park

5) hang out at the shopping mall, go bowling

○ **You are an interviewee. Answer my questions, please.**

A: Excuse me, sir/ma'am.

B: Yes?

A: I'm from CIS Research Inc. May I ask you some questions?

B: Uh, yes, all right.

A: Thank you. First, When do you usually have dinner?

B:

A: What do you usually do after dinner?

B:

A: Do you often see your friends?

B:

A: Do you ever go to the movies?

B:

A: What about the opera? Do you ever go to the opera?

B:

A: Well, thank you.

Describe the followings:

1. A park or a playground you are familiar with;

2. The games popular in Korea;

3. Your favorite beach;

4. Picnics, picnic supplies and food you like;

5. The sports popular in Korea;

6. Favorite teams and famous players in Korea;

7. The most exciting or the most dangerous games in the Winter Olympics.

The Two Brothers

Goals	
Questions	
Task	
Teaching Aids	

Note

Gist of a Lesson

Starting a Lesson		
• Greeting • Warm-Up		
Developing a Lesson		
• Activity 1 • Essential Question 1 • Essential Question 2 • Activity 2 • Essential Question 3 • Essential Question 4 • Activity 3		
Ending a Lesson		
• Wrap-Up		

Once upon a time, there lived two brothers in a small village. The older brother had a round face with big eyes, while the younger brother had an oval face with fair skin. They had different looks but their loving and kind ways to one another were exactly the same.

My story

Scene 2

They took care of their widowed mother, asking about her health every morning and night, serving every meal, and paying their respects to her. Their devotion to their mother was the talk of everyone in the village. After she passed away, they divided the fields their mother gave them. "You are my older brother. You should have more," said the younger brother. The older brother shook his head and suggested the younger brother have more fields. When they spent almost all day dividing their fields, an old man of the village said, "Why don't you work together and divide the sheaves of rice evenly?" They agreed to his idea.

My story

Together they worked very hard all through the day to produce as much as they could from their fields. Every autumn they would have the largest harvest in the village. One day, they spent the whole day dividing up the rice harvest. The older brother said, "You just got married and had many expenses these days. You should have more sheaves." "Not at all," said the younger brother, "You hold memorial services for our ancestors. I know you need more rice to prepare food for the ceremonies."

My story

160

That night, the older brother thought to himself, 'My younger brother needs to buy household goods. I'll put a sack of my rice in his storehouse and not tell him. He will never accept it if I let him know that.' So late that night, he put a sack of rice on his back and carried it to his brother's storeroom. He felt happy.

My story

Scene 5

In the mean time, the younger brother thought to himself, 'My older brother has many kids. Also he prepares food for memorial services. He needs more rice to use.' After a late dinner, he put a sack of rice on his back and carried it to the house of his older brother.

My story

The next morning, while cleaning up his storeroom, the older brother was surprised to find he still had the same number of sacks of rice as he had before. "That's strange," the older brother said, "I put one of my sacks in my younger brother's store house last night. Why do I have the same number? I'll take another one to him tonight." Late that night, he carried another sack of rice to his brother's house.

My story

Scene 7

The next morning, he was again surprised to find he had the same number of sacks as before. He stood confused in his store house and in the end he decided to take another sack to his younger brother. After it gets dark, he loaded the rice sack on his back and set out for his brother's house. It was a full moon and he could see the path quite clearly. And he could see a man carrying something bulky on his back while hurrying down the path in this direction.

My story

"Oh, my brother!" they both called out at the same time. The two brothers put down their sacks and laughed long and hard. It was nothing other than brotherly love that had caused all the confusion. These two brothers lived happily ever after working hard and doing many good things together.

My story

Topic 13　Now and Then
What did you do yesterday?

Goals	**Students can compare life then and life now.**
Questions	• Which do you prefer, life then or life now? • What do you do? What did you do? What are you going to do? • How did our ancestors live?
Task	• Students compare the past life with the present life. • Students identify different tenses. • Students describe the ancestors' lives.
Teaching Aids	퀴즈 자료, 색종이(빨강, 노랑)

Note

동사의 과거형(문법)을 규칙동사와 불규칙동사로 나누어 각각에 해당되는 여러 동사를 암기시키면 적은 시간에 많은 단어를 익히는 듯 보이나 단순기계학습(rote learning)은 유의미 학습(meaningful learning)이 될 수 없으므로 문맥을 통해 익힐 수 있도록 한다.

Gist of a Lesson

Starting a Lesson		
• Greeting • Routine Questions • Checking Attendance • Warm-Up	• 사극과 동시대에 태어났더라면 어땠을지 상상하여 말하기	
Developing a Lesson		
• Activity 1	• Life Then and Life Now 퀴즈 풀어보기 (빈칸을 채우며 과거와 현재의 생활 비교하기)	• 퀴즈 자료
• Essential Question 1	• Which do you prefer, life then or life now? (과거와 현재의 삶을 비교하여 선호하는 것을 말한다.)	
• Activity 2	• Everyday Activities 목록 작성하기 (자신과 친구들의 일상생활 목록 작성하기)	• 빙고 그림
• Essential Question 2	• What do you do? What did you do? What are you going to do?	
• Activity 3	• 익힌 동사를 활용해서 현재, 과거 및 미래시제로 서로 묻고 답하기(미래시제는 '전화영어'를 활용한다.)	
• Essential Question 3	• How did our ancestors live? (우리 조상들의 생활 모습을 이야기한다.)	• 조상들의 생활도구 그림
Ending a Lesson		
• Wrap-Up	• 배운 내용 요약	

Teaching and Learning Plan

Starting a Lesson

T: Hello. Good to see you again.

S: Hello, Teacher.

T: Any good news? You look shiny.

S: Nothing much.

T: Today is Wednesday, isn't it?

S: Yes, it is.

T: Wednesday is in the middle of the weekdays. So sometimes it is called a hump day.

S: A hump day?

T: Yes. Like a hump of a camel.

S: Interesting. A hump day.

T: Uh-huh. What day was it yesterday?

S: It was Tuesday.

T: Good. What day will it be tomorrow?

S: It will be Thursday.

T: Great. Have you ever seen a historical drama like _____ (알 만한 사극의 예를 든다)?

S: Yes.

T: If you were in the drama, I mean if you were born and lived at the same time as the drama, what would happen?

S: 학생들은 사극과 동시대에 태어나 자랐다면 어땠을 지 상상하여 답한다.

T: You would memorize Chinese characters, wear *Hanbok*, have long hair and beard, go to bed early, read books all day, work outside all day, walk or ride horses, etc.
There would be no cars, airplanes, phones, TV sets, radios, computers, Internet, movies, cameras, sneakers, air conditioners, washing machines, refrigerators, etc.

168

Would you be happy?

S: No.

T: Answer to the quiz please.

1) 200 years ago, people <u>washed</u> clothes by hand, but now we use electric(   ).   → washing machines

2) 200 years ago, people <u>traveled</u> on foot or by horse, but now we travel by (   ).   → cars

3) 200 years ago, people <u>sewed</u> by hand, but now we have electric (   ).   → sewing machines

4) 200 years ago, people <u>used</u> oil lamps, but now we have electric (   ).   → lights

5) 200 years ago, people <u>delivered</u> messages in person, but now we use (   ).   → (cellular) phones

6) 200 years ago, people <u>cooked</u> over fires, but now we cook on (   ).   → stoves

7) 200 years ago, people <u>did</u> farming using animals, but now we use (   ).   → farm machines

8) 200 years ago, people <u>cleaned</u> their houses using broomsticks, but now we use (   ).   → vacuum cleaners

9) 200 years ago, people <u>got</u> water from the well, now we get water from the (   ).   → faucet

10) 200 years ago, people <u>had</u> no (,   ,   , etc.) but now we have them all.
    → refrigerators, televisions, cameras, computers, hair dryers, and so on.

S: 학생들은 빈칸에 알맞은 단어를 넣어본다.

→과거와 현재의 삶을 비교할 수 있는 퀴즈를 낸다. 먼저 과거 시제가 있는 과거의 삶을 듣고 그와 반대되는 현대 삶에서 사용하는 물건을 답해본다. 그 다음에는 물건으로 과거의 삶을 유추하여 과거시제를 사용해 보도록 한다.

T: "Which do you prefer, life then or life now?"

S: 학생들은 과거와 오늘날의 삶 중에서 어떤 것을 더 선호하는지 서로서로 이야기 한다.

T: Now I'd like to ask the same question one more time. Which do you prefer, Life Then(the past life) or Life Now(the present life)?

S: I prefer Life Now.

T: What is the reason for you to say that?

S: I cannot live without a computer/a cell phone/video games/comic books/a toilet/movies, etc.

T: I see. It is true our ancestors had no computers, cell phones, or television. But they were wise to live with the nature, in the nature and for the nature. Let's talk about it later.

T: Now let's go back the past again.
(교사는 동사의 과거형을 규칙동사와 불규칙동사라는 용어를 사용하며 직접 설명하지 않고 학생들이 불규칙과 규칙의 개념을 색깔로 이해할 수 있도록 한다.)

→동사의 과거형에 강세를 두어 읽고, 규칙 동사일 경우 노란색을 불규칙 동사일 경우 빨간색을 보여준다.

1) Instead of washing machines, people **washed** clothes by hand.
2) Instead of cars, people **traveled** on foot.
3) Instead of sewing machines, people **sewed** by hand.
4) Instead of lights, people **used** oil lamps.
5) Instead of phones, people **delivered** messaged in person.
6) Instead of stoves, people **cooked** over fires.
7) Instead of farm machines, people **did** farming using animals.
8) Instead of vacuum cleaners, people **cleaned** using broomsticks.
9) Instead of faucet, people **got** water from the well.
10) People **had** no cameras, refrigerators, televisions, computers, hair dryers, and so on.

T: What do you do everyday? Make a list.

S: 학생들은 매일 하는 활동의 목록을 적는다.

T: Interview some friends and make lists of their everyday activities.

S: 친구들의 일과를 묻고 일상 활동의 목록을 작성한다.

활용 어휘

wake up, get up, take a shower, wash my face, get dressed, make the bed, eat breakfast, brush my teeth, brush my hair, comb my hair, go to school, take the bus to school, walk to school, come/get home, study, clean the house, wash the dishes, do the laundry, feed the dog, study, eat dinner, do homework, take out the garbage, read books, watch TV, do exercise, get undressed, go to bed/sleep

➔기본 동사를 익히고 나면, 현재 진행, 과거 및 미래 시제 까지 연습하도록 한다.

T: Work in pairs. Make a list of ten activities.

One student(interviewer) asks, **"What do you do everyday?"**

The other student(interviewee) answers, "I _____."

S: 학생들은 짝 활동으로 하루 일과를 묻고 답한다.

T: Let's change a little bit.

One student(interviewer) asks, **"What did you do yesterday?"**

The other student(interviewee) answers, "I _____."

S: 학생들은 일과를 묻고 답하며 과거 시제 문장 만들기 연습을 한다.

T: Okay. What did you do yesterday?

S: 순서의 정해짐 없이 자유롭게 답변한다.

교사가 특정 학생에게 질문할 수도 있고 답변한 학생이 다른 학생을 지목하여 질문을 던지면 그 학생은 과거시제를 사용하여 답변하는 형식을 반복할 수도 있다.

T: 교사는 학생들의 답변 중 규칙동사의 과거형이 나오면 노란 색지를 불규칙 동사의 과거형이 나오면 빨간 색지를 들어 규칙과 불규칙을 구별한다.

활용 어휘

woke up, got up, took a shower, washed my face, got dressed, made the bed, ate breakfast, brushed my teeth, brushed my hair, combed my hair, went to school, took the bus to school, walked to school, came/got home, studied, cleaned the house, washed the dishes, did the laundry, fed the dog, ate dinner, did homework, took out the garbage, read books, watched TV, did exercise, got undressed, went to bed/sleep

T: Seoyoung, what did you do last weekend?

S1: I **went** to _____. And I _____ there.

→처음 답변한 학생이 그 다음 학생을 지목하여 질문하는 방식을 반복할 수도 있다.

활용 어휘

- a museum(박물관)/the flea market(바자회)/an amusement park(놀이 공원)/ an art gallery(미술관)/the fair(박람회)/the movies(영화관)/a well-known restaurant (이름난 식당)
- I **saw** 유물(artifacts) there.   I **bought** some 물건(items) there.
  I **rode** some 놀이기구(rides).   I **saw** some paintings.
  I **enjoyed** a variety of items and experiences.
  I **saw** a movie.   I **ate** delicious food(음식 이름).

T: Jinny, **"What are you going to do this weekend?"**

S: **I'm going to** go to an art gallery. **I'll** see some paintings.

T: Okay, everyone. Why don't you practice future plans with your partners?

S: 학생들은 앞서 익힌 기본 동사에 'be going to'와 'will'을 넣어 앞으로의 계획을 묻고 답하는 연습을 한다.

→전화를 걸어 상대방이 무엇을 하는지 묻고 답하는 활동도 유익하다. 현재진행형 문장을 연습할 수 있다.

전화 영어

A: Hello, (수신자). This is (발신자).
  What are you doing?

B: I'm cleaning my room. (기본 동사를 진행형으로 바꾼다. be 동사+~ing)
  How about you?

A: I'm feeding fish. Are you going to go to the library soon?

B: Yes. I'm going to go to the library **in a little while**.

A: Then, see you there. Bye.

172

B: Bye.

T: 위와 같은 구문을 제시하여 학생들이 밑줄 친 단어를 바꾸어 대화를 완성하는 연습을 할 수 있도록 한다.

T: Okay. Let's talk about our ancestors' lives more. **"How did our ancestors live?"** They did not have raincoats, apartment houses, or hamburgers. But it does not mean they lived inconvenient and uncomfortable lives. They rather lived well-being lives.

S: Really?

T: They made clothes out of natural material such as skins of animals, bark of plants, silkworms, cotton plant, etc.

S: The ancestors found them and we still use them.

→풀, 나뭇잎, 동물의 가죽, 식물의 껍질, 누에고치, 목화 등의 천연 재료(물질)로 옷을 만들어 입었다.

T: The ancestors made special foods using fresh ingredients of each season. For example, They ate azalea *jeon*(pancakes) in spring, *samgyetang*(chicken broth with ginseng), *songpyeon*(half-moon-shaped rice cake) and *patjuk*(adzuki-bean porridge).

S: We still enjoy these foods.

T: Can you draw the Korean peninsula?
(한반도 지도를 그리며) It looks like this.
The temperature of the Northern part and that of the Southern part is quite different. Which season do the people living in the Northern area prepare for?

S: They prepare for the winter.

T: That's right. How about the Southern region?
Which season do the people living in the Southern region prepare for?

S: They prepare for the summer.

T: Right. So it means people build houses with different shapes and material.

S: They had no concrete or cement?

T: No. They built houses with natural material such as wood, straw, stone, clay, etc.

S: How about the shapes?

T: In the southern region, rooms were arranged in the shaped of '一'.

The house had many windows and doors.

In the central region, rooms were arranged in the shape of 'ㄱ' or 'ㄴ'.

The house had less windows and doors.

In the northern region, rooms were arranged in the shape of 'ㅁ'.

The house had *jeongjugan*-a kitchen connected to a room directly.

Ending a Lesson

T: Today, we thought about 'Life Then and Life Now'. After comparing those lives, we talked about what we prefer. Do you still prefer 'Life Now'?

S: Yes, I do.

T: I see. Then we learned some words about everyday activities. You made a list of your activities, didn't you?

S: Yes, I did.

T: Pretend you are reading a book and answer my questions. What are you doing? I am~ing.

S: I am reading a book.

T: Very good. What did you do yesterday?

S: I read a book.

T: What are you going to do?

S: I am going to read a book.

T: Great. Can you describe our ancestors' lives based on 'food', 'clothing' and 'shelter'?

S: Yes, I can.

T: (과제물을 나누어 주면서)Take one and pass around. This is your homework. You should find some information about these life tools used by our ancestors. Also you should explain when, why and how the tools were used. Okay?

S: Okay.

T: have a nice day! Bye.

S: Bye, Teacher.

To Better Teachers

➲ Ancestors' Well-Being Lives

1. Clothing

1) First clothes were made of natural material including grass, leaves and skins of animals. And then they started to make cloth out of bark of plants, cocoons of silkworms, cotton plants, etc. Also dyeing techniques brought a variety of colors to fabrics.

2) Summer clothes were made out of the following material. What is the answer?

재료		
원료	flax라는 식물의 껍질	ramie라는 식물의 속껍질
특징	올이 거칠고 질기며 바람이 잘 통하고 물에도 강해서 배의 돛, 상복, 미투리 등을 만드는데 쓰였다. 전국적으로 재배된다.	감촉이 깔깔하고 통풍이 잘 되며 습기를 잘 흡수하고 빨리 마른다. 재배 조건이 까다롭기 때문에 생산 지역이 한정되어 있다.

Answer: Linen Fabric(삼베), Ramie Fabric(모시)

3) Winter clothes were made out of the following material.

원료	cotton plant's seed pod	the cocoon of the silkworm
특징	고려 말 공민왕 때 문익점이 씨앗을 들여왔다. 천이 부드럽고 짜는 것과 손질하는 것이 쉬워 사계절 내내 사용되었다.	광택과 촉감이 우수하고 옷감이 매끄럽고 따뜻하다. 그러나 누에치기나 옷감 손질이 어려워 일반 백성이 사용할 수 없는 귀한 옷감이었다.

Answer: Cotton Fabric(무명), Silk Fabric(비단)

2. Food

1) 기온이 높고 습기가 많은 여름철 기후에는 음식이 쉽게 상하는 것을 막기 위해서 소금에 절인 **젓갈**(salted seafood)이나 **장아찌**(jangajji-pickled vegetables) 같은 저장 식품을 먹었고 춥고 건조한 겨울철에는 채소를 재배하기 어려워 **김치를 한꺼번에 담가 두고**(gimjang-making *kimchi* for the winter) 먹었다.

2) 지역별 김치

The climatic differences of each region affected the taste of *kimchi*. In warm places, salted fish and chili powder were used in abundance so that *kimchi* could be prevented from going bad. On the other hand, *kimchi* made in colder areas was less salty and **pungent**.

(남부 지방의 김치는 소금을 많이 넣고, 젓갈을 비롯한 해산물을 많이 넣고, 북부 지방의 김치는 소금을 적게 넣고 양념을 많이 넣지 않아 시원한 맛이 난다.)

3) 김치의 가치

kimchi is an excellent contributor to the human body. *Kimchi* has its own unique nutritional value of promoting health and preventing disease. *Kimchi* is high in fiber, a food component necessary for proper digestion. Also *Kimchi* is rich in minerals, vitamins, calcium and iron, all of which are essential components for human health. *Kimch*i is surprisingly low in calories for a food of such nutritional value, so it provides a great way to lose weight.

(김치는 건강을 증진시켜주고 질병을 막아주는 식품이다. 김치는 건강을 위한 필수 영양소인 섬유질, 무기질, 비타민이, 칼슘, 철이 풍부하며 저칼로리 식품이기 때문에 다이어트에도 효과적이다.)

4) 우리 조상들은 각종 나물(herbs)을 잘 말려 두었다가 다음 제철이 돌아올 때까지 음식을 만들어 먹었다. 또한 각종 세시 음식(a variety of seasonal food)을 만들어 이웃과 나누어 먹음으로써 공동의 행복(public happiness)과 안녕(well-being)을 추구하였다.

3. House

1) '일(一)'자 모양의 집 구조('一'-shaped house structure)를 가지고 있고 넓은 마루 (a wide wooden floor)가 발달했으며 창문과 방문이 많은 것은 남부 지방(the southern region)의 집이고, 남부 지방에 비해서는 마루가 좁고 창문이 적으며 'ㄱ'자 모양의 집 구조('ㄱ'-shaped house structure)를 가지고 있는 것은 중부 지 방(the central region)의 집이고요 추운 날씨에 대비하기 위해 방들이 서로 붙어 있고 마루가 없으며 방과 부엌 사이에 *정주간(jeongjugan*-a kitchen connecting a cooking fireplace to a room without any walls)이 있으며 'ㅁ'자 모양의 집('ㅁ'-shaped houses)을 지은 것은 북부 지방(the northern region)이다.

2) 한옥에는 조상의 슬기가 담겨 있는데, 이것은 추위를 이겨내기 위해 만든 난방 장 치이다. 방바닥 밑에 넓고 편평한 돌을 놓아, 아궁이에서 불을 지필 때 생긴 열기 가 돌로 옮겨 가서 방바닥 전체에 퍼지도록 하였다. 이것은 무엇인가?

Traditional floors were heated by channeling warm air and smoke through a system of under-the-floor flues from an exterior fireplace. Those floors typically were made of large pieces of flat stone tightly covered with several square-yard-size pieces of lacquered paper in light golden brown to present an aesthetically pleasing surface and prevent gas and smoke from entering the room.

온돌(ondol)

3) 여름철 무더운 날씨를 견디기 위해 방과 방 사이에 바람이 잘 통하도록 이것을 놓았는데, 오늘날의 거실이 이 역할을 대신하고 있습니다. 이것은 무엇인가?

마루(a wooden floor)

4) 한옥(Korean-style house)의 재료는 자연에서 얻을 수 있는 나무(wood)와 짚(straw), 흙(clay)으로 만들어 공해(pollution)가 없고, 방바닥이나 벽을 황토(red clay)로 발라 건강에도 좋다.

Worksheet

➔ Our ancestors made and used the following life tools. Write down the uses.

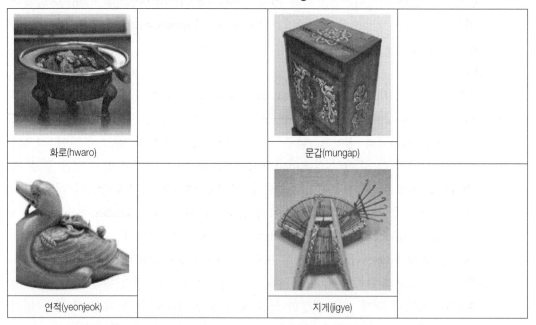

화로(hwaro)		문갑(mungap)	
연적(yeonjeok)		지게(jigye)	

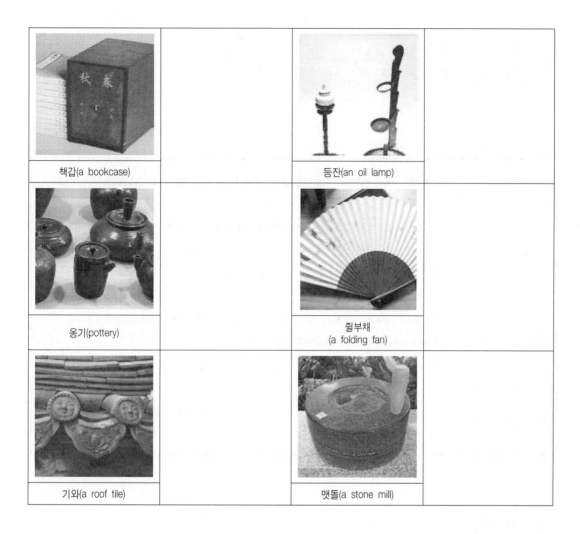

책갑(a bookcase)		등잔(an oil lamp)
옹기(pottery)		쥘부채 (a folding fan)
기와(a roof tile)		맷돌(a stone mill)

Nature
Let's protect the environment.

Goals	**Students understand the nature and how to protect the environment.**
Questions	• What can you do to protect the environment? • What lives on the Earth except human beings? • How can we survive natural disasters?
Task	• Students talk about what they can do for environment. • Students identify animals and plants. • Students describe the way to survive natural disasters.
Teaching Aids	map or globe(지도나 지구본), photos of animals and plants(동식물 사진)

Note

흔히 동물원이 나오면 그 곳에서 볼 수 있는 동물에 대해 열거하고 가장 좋아하는 동물이나 싫어하는 동물로 끝나는 경우가 많은데 이 장에서는 '자연'이라는 주제를 가지고 동물, 식물, 자연재해, 환경보존을 위해 우리가 할 수 있는 일에 대해 이야기해본다.

Gist of a Lesson

Starting a Lesson		
■ Greeting ■ Routine Questions ■ Checking Attendance ■ Warm-Up	 ■ 과자 봉지 등으로 더러워진 교실을 지적한다.	
Developing a Lesson		
■ Essential Question 1 ■ Essential Question 2 ■ Activity 1 ■ Activity 2 ■ Essential Question 3	■ What can you do to protect the environment? (환경보존을 위해 할 수 있는 일에 대해 이야기한다.) ■ What lives on Earth except human beings? (인간 외에 지구에 살고 있는 것에 대해 이야기한다.) ■ 좋아 하는 동물이 되어보기 (동물의 관점에서 환경오염에 대한 이야기를 한다.) ■ 식물 이름 알기 (대화를 완성하면서 나무와 꽃의 이름을 익힌다. 특별한 날에 사용하는 꽃에 대해 이야기 한다.) ■ How can we survive natural disasters? (자연재해로부터의 생존 방법에 대한 이야기를 한다.)	● 동물사진, 지구본 혹은 지도 ● 대화 구문
Ending a Lesson		
■ Wrap-Up	■ 배운 내용 요약	

181

Teaching and Learning Plan

T: Hi, students.

S: Hello, Teacher.

T: It's always good to see you again. How about you?

S: Me, too.

T: Isn't it cold nowadays?

S: Yes, it is.

T: Look at the sky. It seems like we have snow today.

S: That's good. I hope so.

T: Tell me the date, please.

S: Today is November 11th.

T: You are giving and taking 'stick cookies' today?

S: Yes.

T: You must be busy eating them. Look at the floor. Empty packages and boxes.

S: I'm sorry.

T: Last week we talked about the Earth in the solar system. It is the only planet with people, animals, plants, air, earth and water. Do you remember?

S: Yes, I do.

Developing a Lesson

T: Have you heard about **Earth Day**(지구의 날)?

S: No. When is the Earth Day?

T: It is April 22.

S: I didn't know.

T: Earth is the only place our ancestors lived, now we are living

182

and our descendants will live. It is needless to say that the earth is so precious and essential, isn't it?

S: Yes, it is.

T: Many people worry about environmental problems such as **air pollution, water pollution, dangerous waste, acid rain, radiation, global warming**, etc. They suggest we protect the environment. Do you agree with them?

S: Yes, I do. I am concerned about the environment.

T: So **"What can you do to protect the environment?"**

S: 학생들은 환경보존을 위해 할 수 있는 일에 대해 의논한다.

➡학생들이 실천할 수 있는 일에 관해 이야기한다.

활용 표현

- I can save energy.
   1) I turn off the lights when I leave the room.
   2) I turn off the TV when I finish watching it.
- I can keep air clean.
   1) I can ride my bike or walk to school.
   2) Too many cars cause air pollution.
- I can save water and keep it clean.
   1) I don't leave the water running while I brush my teeth.
   2) Too much detergent causes water pollution.
- I can save paper and protect trees.
   1) I use both sides of paper at school and at home.
   2) I reduce disposable paper use.
- I can keep our neighborhood clean.
   1) I pick up litter and throw it in the trash can.
   2) I recycle cans, bottles, newspapers and magazines.

T: You do care about the environment.

The nature does not belong to us. We belong to the nature.

"What lives on Earth except human beings?"

S: Animals and plants.

T: Let's talk about the animals first. How can we sort animals?

S: Places they live, food they eat, sizes and shapes.

T: Okay. Then we can talk about the places they live. First, tell me some animals living in African plains.

(교사는 특정 지역을 선택하여 그 곳에 어떤 동물이 살고 있는지 묻는다.)

S: Lions, zebras, giraffes, elephants.......

(학생들은 교사의 질문에 대한 답을 한국어로 할 수 있으며 교사는 아래의 어휘를 활용하여 영어로 바꾸어 준다.)

활용 어휘

- Animals living in African plains(아프리카 평원의 동물): leopards, cheetahs, hyenas, hippopotamuses, rhinoceroses, ostriches, buffalos, flamingoes, etc.
- Animals living in Tropical Rainforests(열대우림지역의 동물): tigers, jaguars, monkeys, orangutangs, (toucans, parrots), (piranhas), (tarantulas), etc.
- Animals living Polar Regions(극지역의 동물): polar bears, mooses, arctic foxes, reindeer, penguins, puffins, huskies, walruses, seals, etc.
- Animals living in Deserts(사막의 동물): camels, gazelles, bats, (vultures, eagles), (lizards), (rattlesnakes), scorpions, etc.
- Animals living in Australian Outback(호주오지의 동물): kangaroos, emus, wombats, dingoes, koalas, platypuses, (kookaburras), (crocodiles), etc.

T: What animals can we see in Korea?

S: 학생들은 한국에서 볼 수 있는 동물에 대해 이야기 한다.

T: If you could be an animal, which animal would you like to be?

S1: My favorite animal is a puppy. I would like to be a puppy.

T: Good. Now Imagine you are an animal. It doesn't matter which animal you choose. Talk with your partners about environmental problems in your point of view.

S2: I am a dolphin. I am living in the sea. Do you know I am smart?

S: Yes, I do.

S2: But I cannot say which one is food and which one is garbage.

➜ ❶동물/식물/곤충 그림이나 카드를 펼쳐놓고 사는 지역별로 분류해 본다. ❷ 포유류, 양서류, 파충류, 어류, 곤충, 식물로 분류해 본다. ❸ 수업 공간은 지구가 되고 학생들은 동물이 되어 사는 지역을 찾아 간다.

➜동물 되어보기 활동을 할 때 학생들은 자신의 이름(동물)과 사는 곳을 먼저 소개한다. 예를 들어 'Hello, I'm Polar bear. Nice to meet you. I am living near the North Pole. Nowadays the glaciers are melting because of global warming. We have less places to move or stay.'

Some of my friends died because they ate harmful waste people deserted.

T: Is it dangerous to live in the sea?

S2: Yes, it is. It is very dirty and messy with lots of waste.

T: Then tell us what we should do.

S2: Do not dump in the sea.

T: Okay. Thank you. We should protect the sea.

S3: I am a sparrow. It is dangerous to fly in the air.

T: What's the matter?

S3: The air is full of dirty and harmful smoke from the factories, cars, fires, etc.

T: I am sorry to hear that.

S4: I am a mole. The earth stink 'cause people dump and bury waste. Animals and plants are losing their places because of waste.

T: That's why animals and plants have many diseases.

S: 학생들은 동물이 되어 자신들의 입장에서 환경오염의 문제점에 관해 이야기 한다.

➛대화 구문을 활용하여 나무와 꽃의 이름을 익힌다.

➛어버이날, 스승의 날, 생일, 성년식, 결혼식, 장례식에 어떤 꽃이 사용되는지 이야기 해 본다.

T: Okay. Now let's talk about plants. What kinds of trees and flowers do you know? What is your favorite tree or flower?

S: 학생들은 자신이 알고 있거나 좋아하는 나무와 꽃에 대해 이야기 한다.

T: Which flower do people use for different occasions such as parents/teachers days, birthdays, coming-of-age day, weddings, funerals, etc.

S: 학생들은 특별한 상황에서 사용하는 꽃에 대해 이야기 한다.

- **A:** What kind of tree is that?
  B: I think it a/an _____ tree.
- **A:** Look at all the _____s.
  B: They're so beautiful.

birch(자작나무)	cherry(벚나무)	dogwood(층층나무)	elm(느릅나무)
holly(호랑가시나무)	magnolia(목련나무)	maple(단풍나무)	oak(참나무)
palm(야자나무)	pine(잣나무)	willow(버드나무)	azalea(진달래)
carnation(카네이션)	cosmos(코스모스)	daffodil(수선화)	daisy(데이지)
forsithia(개나리)	geranium(제라늄)	iris(붓꽃)	jasmine(재스민)

lily(백합)	marigold(금잔화)	pansy(팬지)	petunia(페튜니아)
poinsettia(포인세티아)	sunflower(해바라기)	chrysanthemum(국화)	violet(제비꽃)

T: Human beings, animals, trees and flowers belong to nature. We are from Mother Nature. But sometimes we suffer from natural disasters. Did you hear about the tsunami in Japan?

S: Yes, I did. I saw it on the news.

T: It was dreadful. The tsunami killed so many people and animals, destructed buildings, houses and fields. It caused horrible situations.

Any natural disasters you experienced or saw on the news?

S: 학생들은 자신이 경험했거나 뉴스에서 본 자연재해에 관해 이야기 한다.

→ 모둠별로 자연재해 중 한 가지를 선택해 대피요령을 조사해서 발표하도록 하는 것이 효과적이다.

활용 구문

- I saw the_____ in _____ (country/region/city).
- avalanche(눈사태), blizzard(폭풍설, 심한 눈보라), drought(가뭄), earthquake(지진), flood(홍수), forest fire(산불), hurricane(대폭풍, 허리케인), landslide(산사태), tornado(토네이도), tsunami(쓰나미, 지진에 의한 해일), typhoon(태풍), volcano eruption(화산 폭발),

T: Which natural disasters sometimes happen in Korea?

S: Earthquakes, floods and typhoons.

T: What should we do to survive the earthquake?

S1: If you are in a building, you should get away from windows and get under a table.

S2: Cover your head and neck. You should not move until the shaking has stopped.

T: Right. Aftershocks(여진) are possible.

S3: Get out of the building slowly and meet your family or other people.

S4: Inspect the building for anything dangerous and stay away from damaged areas.

S5: We should be very careful when we turn on the electrical devices(전기제품).

S6: Also we should not drink any water from the tap and flush the toilet. Also we should open the cabinets very cautiously.

S7: If you are outdoors, you should move away from buildings, seek shelter and stay there for around 20 seconds. Use cautions and come out of the shelter. Remember to wait a minute or two.

T: Wow. Your group's information is very useful. We have to remember that. Thank you very much. And how about flood? What should we do?

S8: First pay attention to flood warnings. Prepare Emergency Kit.

T: What's inside the emergency kit?

S9: First aid kit, bottled water, canned food, wet wipes, flash light, radio, protective clothing, sleeping bag, etc.

S10: During a flood, you should leave the house or building immediately.

Move to higher ground away from rivers or streams.

T: Thank you. It is very important to act quickly during a flood. Now let's talk about typhoon. What should we do to survive typhoon?

S11: Before the typhoon strikes, you should prepare Emergency Kit. Put packing tape across the windows. They may break into pieces.

And turn off the power except for the refrigerator.

S12: During the storm, stay inside. The greatest danger is flying objects like signs, tree limbs and other objects. Sit far away from the windows in case they break.

S13: After the typhoon, survey your house and check on your neighbors to see if they are okay. Watch for downed power lines and contaminated water.

T: Thank you for your instructions. Well done, everyone.

Ending a Lesson

T: Today, we talked about nature. There are lots of creatures living in the nature. And the most important thing is we live together. Did you learn some new vocabulary about animals, trees and flowers?

S: Yes, I did. The new words were ....

T: To protect the environment is not optional but compulsory. Do you agree with that?

S: Yes, I do.

T: What can you do protect the environment?

S: I can practice saving. I can save water, paper, pencils, energy, etc.

T: Anything else?

S: I can walk to school. Also I do not dump waste.

T: Right. I hope you practice what you can do.
And we talked about natural disasters. Which natural disasters sometimes happen in Korean?

S: Floods, typhoons and earthquakes happen in Korea.

T: What should we do during those disasters?

S: We should get emergency kit and find a shelter.

T: Should wait until the official announcement says we are safe?

S: Yes, of course.

T: It's almost time to finish. You did a perfect job. I appreciate that. Thank you, everyone. See you next time. Bye.

S: Thank you. Bye, Teacher.

To Better Teachers

➲ Fill in the blanks.

I can draw and color on _____ sides of my paper. I must remember to turn _____ the lights when I leave an empty room. This saves _____. I can also _____ up litter on the ground and put it in the _____ can. It is important that I help _____ cans, bottles and newspapers. When I ride my bike or walk to school, I don't _____ the air. I am important! I can _____ save the environment.

Answers: both, off, energy, pick, trash, recycle, pollute, help

➲ Choose the proper word in the box and complete each sentence.

animals, healthy, tree, juice box, lights, shower, cans, recycle, TV, water, lunch box

1. Don't leave the _____ running when you are brushing your teeth.
2. Take a _____ instead of a bath.
3. If you litter, _____ will eat the garbage and get sick.
4. We can _____ by using both sides of the paper.
5. Use a reusable juice container instead of a _____.
6. Planting just one _____ can save the sky from smoke from factories.
7. Turn off the _____ and _____ when you are not in the room.
8. Keep the oceans clean so the fish will stay _____ and safe.
9. Recycle your plastic and _____ .
10. Use a _____ instead of a paper bag.

➲ Read the questions carefully and answer them.

1. This word starts with a "P." It is the name of a large object in space that orbits the Sun. The Earth is the only one of these on which we can live. What is it?

   _____

   planet

2. This word starts with an "E." It is the word that describes our surroundings - the air we breathe, the water, plants, animals and the Earth itself. What is it?

_____

environment

3. This phrase starts with an "E." Many plant and animal groups are close to becoming extinct. What is the word that describes them? _____

endangered species

4. This word starts with an "E." We get most of this directly from the Sun, but we also generate it using coal, nuclear generators, hydro-electric plants, and the wind. What is it? _____

energy

5. This word starts with an "R." When we re-use items, we can help the environment. Used paper can be made into new paper, metals and glass can be re-used also. What is the term for this? _____

recycling

6. This word starts with an "R." It is a warm, moist area that is rich in plant and animal life. This biome is important for the health of the entire Earth. What is it?

_____

rainforest

7. This word starts with an "A." It is a type of polluted precipitation (moisture falling from the sky) that causes erosion and corrosion. What is it? _____

acid rain

8. This word starts with an "A." It is another name for the air that surrounds the Earth. What is it? _____

atmosphere

9. This word starts with a "W." It is a very important substance for all living things. When it becomes polluted, many living things suffer. What is it? _____

water

10. This phrase starts with a "W." It is the name of a process that recirculates an important substance from the Earth to the sky and back again. What is it?

_____

water cycle

11. This word starts with a "W." It is the name of the state that the outdoors is in, like how hot or cold it is, or if it is raining or snowing. What is it?

_____

weather

12. This word starts with a "W." It is the name for animals and plants that live in

their natural habitat. What is it? _____

13. This word starts with a "C." It is a rich, soil-like substance that is formed when we recycle plant material. What is it? _____

14. This word starts with an "H." It is the type of place where a plant or animal lives. What is it? _____

15. This word starts with a "B." It is the name for the natural environment in a particular climate where many plants and animals live. What is it?

_____

Subjects
I love English.

Goals	**Students can understand main vocabulary about subjects.**
Questions	• What is your favorite subject? Why do you like it? • What is the most important and useful subject? Why do you think so?
Task	• Students identify words about P.E. and express them with gestures. • Students identify musical instruments and their positions in the orchestra. • Students describe the kinds of writing(literature) and the planets in the solar system.
Teaching Aids	체육용어 단어카드, 관현악단 악기 배치 그림, 다양한 글의 종류 복사본, 행성 그림

Note

학교에서 다루는 여러 교과의 주요 개념을 영어로 이해시키는 것은 보통의 영어 수업에서 거의 불가능하다. 과목의 종류와 그 과목의 특정 부분과 관련된 어휘를 여러 활동을 통해 익힐 수 있도록 한다.

Gist of a Lesson

Starting a Lesson		
▪ Greeting ▪ Routine Questions ▪ Checking Attendance ▪ Warm-Up	▪ 특정 요일에 어떤 과목을 배우는지 시간표를 묻는다.	
Developing a Lesson		
▪ Essential Question 1	▪ What is your favorite subject? Why do you like it?	
▪ Activity 1	▪ 체육용어 익히기 (동작으로 단어 설명하기)	● 단어 카드
▪ Activity 2	▪ 관현악 연주에서 각 악기의 위치 알기 (학생 자신이 악기가 되어 지휘자를 중심으로 자리 잡기)	● 악기 위치 그림
▪ Activity 3	▪ 글의 종류 알기 (교사가 나누어 주는 글이 어떤 종류에 속하는지 파악하고 몇 가지 단어를 바꾸어 내용을 변경한다)	● 다양한 종류의 글
▪ Activity 4	▪ 행성 놀이 (각자가 행성이 되어 태양 주위를 돌려 챈트 하기)	● 행성& 챈트 카드
▪ Essential Question 2	▪ What is the most important and useful subject? Why do you think so?	
Ending a Lesson		
▪ Wrap-Up	▪ 배운 내용 요약	

Teaching and Learning Plan

Starting a Lesson

T: Hello, everyone.

S: Hello.

T: How's everything going?

S: Pretty good.

T: What day is it today?

S: It's a hump day.

T: You have good memory. What's the date today?

S: It's December 1st.

T: Oh. The last month of the year starts.
(학생들을 둘러보며) Is everyone here?

S: Yes.

T: How many classes do you have today?

S: Four classes.

T: What are they?

S: (They are) Korean, mathematics, sociology and home economics.

Developing a Lesson

T: **"What is your favorite subject? Why do you like it?"**

S: 학생들은 자신이 어떤 과목을 좋아하고 그 이유는 무엇인지 이야기한다.

활용 어휘

- 교과목: Korean, math, sociology(history, geography, government), science (biology, chemistry, physics, health), ethics, home economics(computer), music, art, foreign language(English, Chinese, Japanese), P.E.(physical education)

➤질문은 다음과 같이 바꿔 볼 수도 있다.
"What is the most interesting subject?" 또는 "What is the most difficult subject?" "Why do you think so?"

T: It's quite interesting most of you like P.E. And the reason is you don't have to take notes or cram for an exam.

S: I wish to play dodge ball all day.

T: Okay. Let's play a game. It's not dodge ball you like, but it will be fun.

Let me explain how to do it.

I'll divide you into three groups. Each group stands in one line. Except the first person, the others turn around and face the back. The first person reads the word I show and pats the next person on the shoulder. When the next person turns around, the first person explains it with gestures, not words. The second person does the same thing to the third person and it goes on and on to the last person. The last one should say the action.

S: 학생들은 그룹 별로 한 줄 서기를 한다. 한 그룹 먼저 게임을 시작한다. 첫 번째 사람을 제외하고 나머지 학생들은 뒤로 돌아선다. 첫 번째 학생이 교사가 보여주는 단어를 그 다음 사람에게 말이 아닌 동작으로 설명한다. 두 번째 학생은 첫 번째 학생이 어깨를 두드릴 때에만 뒤돌아 볼 수 있다. 두 번째 학생도 같은 방식으로 세 번째 학생에게 설명하며 맨 마지막에 서있는 학생이 어떤 단어인지 말한다. 시간은 1~3분을 주며 그 동안에 많은 답을 맞힌 팀이 이긴다. 첫 번째 학생은 그 줄의 맨 마지막으로 이동한다.

➔한 그룹이 게임을 진행하는 동안 나머지 그룹의 학생들은 다른 그룹의 게임을 감상 및 규칙을 지키는지 (답을 제외하고 모든 설명은 동작으로 하며 자신의 차례가 될 때까지 눈을 감고 뒤돌아보지 않기) 확인한다.

(**활용 어휘**)

P.E. vocabulary
- ~ the ball: pitch, throw, hit, catch, pass, kick, serve, bounce, dribble, shoot
- walk, run, jump, hop, skip, stretch, bend, reach, swing, lift
- do a ~ : push-up, sit-up, jumping jack(PT체조), forward roll, backward roll, somersault(공중제비 돌기), cartwheel(풍차 돌기), handstand(물구나무 서기)

T: Was it fun? Good.

Now look at this picture.

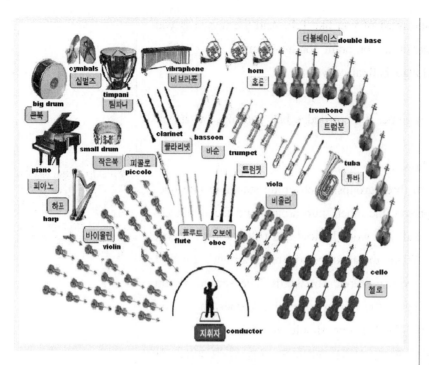

T: This picture shows musical instruments and their position in the orchestra. Look carefully at the instruments and their position.

S: 학생들은 악기 이름과 위치를 익힌다.

T: Now come out to the front and pick one slip of paper in the box. You are now the instrument on the paper. Find the correct position of the instrument in the orchestra. Now I am the conductor.

S: 학생들은 관현악단의 악기 위치를 찾아간다.

S1: (바이올린 연주를 흉내 내며) I am the violin.

S2: (바이올린 연주를 흉내 내며) I am the violin, too.

S: 바이올린이 올바른 위치에 모여 "We are violins"라 하면 다른 학생들이 박수를 친다.

S3: (자리에 앉아 트롬본 연주를 흉내 내며) I am the trumpet.

S: No.

S3: (트럼펫 연주를 흉내 내며) Oh, I am the trumpet.

S: 박수를 친다.

➤교사가 악기 이름을 적어 둔 미션쪽지를 아이들이 고르도록 한다. 지휘자인 교사를 기준으로 아이들은 자신의 위치를 찾아간다. 악기를 연주하는 동작을 취하며 악기 이름을 말했을 때 맞으면 모두가 박수를 쳐준다. 같은 악기를 찾아 함께 이동하는 것이 더 재미있다.

Musical Instruments
- strings(현악기): violin, viola, cello, double bass, guitar, electric guitar, harp
- woodwinds(목관악기): piccolo, flute, oboe, clarinet, recorder, bassoon, saxophone
- brass(금관악기): trumpet, trombone, horn, tuba
- percussion(타악기): drums, cymbals, tambourine, vibraphone, xylophone, timpani
- piano, accordion, harmonica

T: What kinds of literature(books) do you like?

Do you like picture books(그림책), poetry(시집) or novels(소설책)?

S: Comic books.

T: Oh I missed them. I like comic books as well.

I made copies of different kinds of literature and writing.

Get one and pass them around.

Read your writing and label it according to the kinds on the board.

S: 학생들은 본인이 가지고 있는 글을 읽고 어떤 종류에 해당되는지 표시한다.

T: Here are some types of literature and writing.

필수 어휘

poetry/poem(시), novel(소설), biography(전기), autobiography(자서전), essay(수필), report(보고서), magazine article(잡지 기사), newspaper article(신문 기사), editorial(사설), letter(편지), postcard(엽서), note(짧은 편지/쪽지), invitation(초대), thank you note(감사편지), memo(비망록), e-mail(전자우편), Internet message(인터넷 메시지), text message(문자 메시지), diary(일기)

T: Did you label the writing you have? Good. How about writing something to have the same label? You can write three to five sentences.

→교사는 필수어휘를 보드에 적어두거나 다른 방식으로 학생들에게 제시하여, 학생들이 자신들이 가지고 있는 글의 종류를 표시할 수 있도록 한다.

S: 학생들은 자신이 가지고 있는 글의 종류를 이해하고 단어를 바꾸어 글의 내용을 바꾸어 본다.

'긍정문'은 '부정문'으로 '운동을 합시다!'는 '컴퓨터 게임을 합시다!'로 바뀔 수 있기 때문에 모두가 즐거운 시간을 보낼 수 있다.

T: It was fun. Well are you good at mental calculation(암산)?

S: Mental calculation? Not sure.

T: Let's see. 2 **plus** 4 equals?

S: 6.

T: 10 **minus** 5 equals?

S: 5.

T: 2 **times** 3 equals?

S: 6.

T: 8 **divided by** 4 equals?

S: 2.

T: I think you're genius.

S: (Laughing) I think so.

T: Now let's go to the space. Shall we go together?

S: Yes.

T: Pick one of these cards. You will see one of eight planets in the solar system. When you turn the card over, you will see the planet chant. Students with the same planet gather together and practice the chant, please.

S: 학생들은 8개의 행성 중 하나가 된다.

T: I am the sun. The first planet from the sun is Mercury(수성). If you have Mercury on your card, come here. The second planet is Venus(금성). You have Venus on your card? Come here. The next one is Earth. Come together here. The fourth one is Mars. And the fifth one is Jupiter. The next one is Saturn. The seventh one is Uranus. The last one is Neptune. Students with Neptune,

➔ 4칙연산
◆ 덧셈(addition)
  : add
◆ 뺄셈(subtraction)
  : subtract
◆ 곱셈(multiplication)
  : multiply
◆ 나눗셈(division)
  : divide

stand over there.

S: 같은 행성 이름을 가진 학생들은 교사를 기준으로 각각 순서대로 모여서 챈트를 읽어본다.

T: Are you ready to move chanting your planet? Mercury, go!

S: 수성 먼저 태양 궤도 돌며 챈트한다. 박수를 치면서 해도 좋다. 다른 행성은 각자의 위치에서 대기하거나 궤도를 따라 이동해도 좋다. 수성에서 해왕성까지 각 행성별 챈트가 끝나면 학생들 모두 동시에 각자의 챈트와 함께 태양의 주위를 공전한다.

➜학생들은 자신의 궤도를 이탈하지 않고 태양의 주위를 공전한다. 챈트를 암기해서 하면 박수를 치면서 이동할 수 있어서 더욱 재미있다.

행성별 챈트

Mercury

Planet number one is the closest to the Sun.
And Mercury, Mercury, Mercury is its name.
It's a tiny little spot with a surface that's so hot.
And a metal's got a name that's the same.

Venus

Planet number two is an easy one to view.
And Venus, bright Venus, Venus is its name.
Venus is the same as the goddess with that name.
She's a beauty of a planet you will agree.

Earth

Planet number three is the place for you and me.
And Earth, Earth is the planet we call home.
It's got air, water and some land for us all.
Yes, Earth is the place we call our own.

Mars

Planet number five is a reddish colored one.
And Mars, Mars, Mars is its name.

Nights and days are a lot like ours.

A neighbor with two moons is pretty close to home.

Jupiter

Planet number five is the biggest one we see.

And Jupiter, Jupiter, Jupiter is its name.

With a big red spot on its face.

It's a spinning ball of gas, and going round so fast.

Saturn

Planet number six has really got some tricks.

And Saturn, Saturn, Saturn is its name.

The really special thing is the famous rings.

It's a sight to see but a telescopic treat.

Uranus

Planet number seven makes you want to jump and shout.

And Uranus, Uranus, Uranus is its name.

Uranus is big, big and blue.

It's spinning on its side and that's very weird.

Neptune

Planets number eight plays a game often.

And Neptune, Neptune, Neptune is its name.

It's far from the Sun and it's really hard to see.

It changes its place along the way.

T: Well done, everyone. Now look at this picture and compare the sizes.

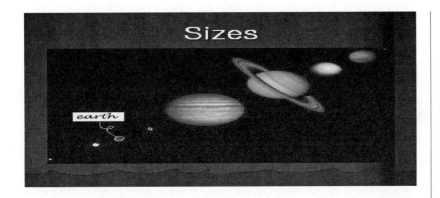

Is the earth bigger than other planets?

S: No. It is very small.

T: It is bigger than Mercury, Venus and Mars, but it is much smaller than Jupiter, Saturn, Uranus and Neptune.

But do you agree it is the most important planet in the universe?

S: Yes, of course.

T: Now tell me **"what is the most important and useful subject? Why do you think so?"**

S: 학생들은 자신이 생각하는 가장 중요하고 유용한 과목에 대해 이야기 한다.

(활용 표현)

- We can enjoy more convenient and comfortable lives thanks to science.
- Korean is the culture of Korea. As we are Koreans, we have responsibility for keeping it and handing it down to next generations.
- Music and art make us better and nicer.
- We can be healthier through P.E.
- Mathematics makes us more logical and reasonable.

T: Thank you everyone. Every subject is important according to your opinions. I hope you enjoy every subject and understand the main idea.

Ending a Lesson

T: Today we talked about favorite subjects and learned some words about several subjects.

Did you enjoy activities?

S: Yes, I did.

T: Good. The words we met today do not mean the subjects themselves.

When you learn each subject, you should try to understand the idea.

Do you understand what I mean?

S: Yes, I do.

T: Also we talked about the most important and useful subjects. Everyone has different values and world views, so the answers are different.

I just wish you to enjoy every subject at school. Okay?

S: Okay.

T: Well done, everyone. Have a good day!

S: You, too. Bye.

To Better Teachers

⊃ Understanding the Solar System

1. Features

● Mercury

Mercury is a rocky sphere. It rotates slowly, so its days are very long. If you lived on Mercury, one day would be equal to 59 days on Earth.

● Venus

Venus's temperature is blistering hot at 864°F(462°C). Thick poisonous clouds block out the sun. It's dark and gloomy.

● Earth

It is the only place where life is known to exist. About 71% of the surface is covered with salt-water oceans and the remainder consists of continents, islands and liquid water.

● Mars

l The red color of Mars comes from the iron-rich dust of its surface. If you weighed 100 pounds on Earth, you would weigh only 38 pounds on Mars.

● Jupiter

It is a hot ball of gas and liquid. It's so large that 1,300 Earths could fit inside. It is now known that Jupiter has thin rings around it and sixteen moons. The largest moon is bigger than Mercury.

● Saturn

It is very windy on Saturn. The temperature is -288°F(-142°C). Saturn's seven rings are made of billions of pieces of ice.

● Uranus

It is the coldest planet in the Solar System. The temperature is -435°F(-224°C). Uranus has a ring system and numerous moons. The wind speeds can reach 250 meters per second.

● Neptune

l It is the farthest planet from the sun. Uranus and Neptune look blue because of the gases in their atmosphere. It has the strongest winds, measured as high as 2,100 kilometers per hour.

2. Sizes

If the Earth were as large as an **onion**, Mercury would be the size of **pea**. Venus would be the size of **walnut**. Mars would be the size of **cherry**. Jupiter would be the size of a large head of **lettuce**. Saturn would be the size of a **grapefruit**. Uranus would be the size of a small head of **lettuce**. Neptune would be the size of an **orange**.

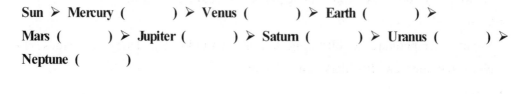

Sun ➤ Mercury (   ) ➤ Venus (   ) ➤ Earth (   ) ➤ Mars (   ) ➤ Jupiter (   ) ➤ Saturn (   ) ➤ Uranus (   ) ➤ Neptune (   )

3. Distance

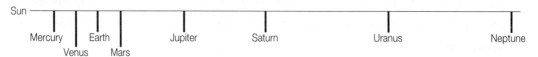

If the Earth were **2.5** centimeters from the sun, Mercury would be about **0.8** centimeters from the sun. Venus would be about **1.9** centimeters from the sun. Mars would be about **3.75** centimeters from the sun. Jupiter would be about **13.75** centimeters from the sun. Saturn would be about **23.75** centimeters from the sun. Uranus would be about **48.75** centimeters from the sun. Neptune would be about **75** centimeters from the sun.

➲ Understanding English Composition

1. Types of Sentences
- declarative sentence(평서문): A cube has six squares.
- interrogative sentence(의문문): How many triangles does a pyramid have?
- imperative sentence(명령문): Draw a cylinder.
- exclamatory sentence(감탄문): What a big cone it is!

2. Parts of Speech(품사)

noun(명사), pronoun(대명사), verb(동사), adjective(형용사), adverb(부사),

preposition(전치사), conjunction(접속사), exclamation/interjection(감탄사)

3. Put Punctuation Marks in the blanks.
period/dot(   ), question mark(   ), exclamation mark/point(   ),
comma(   ), apostrophe(   ), single quotation mark(   ),
double quotation mark(   ), colon(   ), semi-colon(   )

4. Writing Process
   1) Brainstorm ideas.
   2) Organize the ideas.
   3) Write a first draft including a title and a paragraph.
   4) Make corrections. Revise and Edit.
   5) Get feedback.
   6) Write a final copy. Rewrite.

The Snail Lady

Goals	
Questions	
Task	
Teaching Aids	

Gist of a Lesson

Starting a Lesson		
▪ Greeting ▪ Warm-Up		
Developing a Lesson		
▪ Activity 1 ▪ Essential Question 1 ▪ Essential Question 2 ▪ Activity 2 ▪ Essential Question 3 ▪ Essential Question 4 ▪ Activity 3		
Ending a Lesson		
▪ Wrap-Up		

Scene 1

Once there was a young man who lived all alone in a small village. One day while he was tilling his rice field, he muttered to himself, "Everyday I plow the field. But who do I share my meals with? I'm tired of eating alone." Then he heard the woman's voice. "Share your meals with me." Very surprised, he looked all around but saw no one. The young man repeated what he said, "My job is to till the field and harvest crops. Everyday I plow the field. But who do I share my meals with?" "Share your meals with me," said the same voice. The voice came from somewhere close by. All he saw was a small snail. He picked up the snail and put it in a big clay jar.

My story

209

Next morning he was surprised to find a delicious breakfast waiting for him. There was even a lunch box filled with yummy food. He looked all through the house but could not see anyone. He went out to work in the field. That evening another meal lay on the table prepared for the young man. Next morning he found breakfast set on the table and saw supper when he came back home in the evening. This weird thing happens everyday. 'Who makes me these nice meals everyday?' the young man thought to himself.

My story

Scene 3

One day he pretended to go out to work in the field but quietly tiptoed back. Hiding near the house, he peeped into the kitchen. "Oh my goodness!" he couldn't believe what he saw. A beautiful woman stepped out of the clay jar where he had put the snail. She cleaned the house, washed his clothes and mended some of his old clothing. After she prepared his dinner, she turned into a snail and crawled back into the jar. As he stared in amazement, he thought to himself, 'How I wish that beautiful lady were my wife.' The next morning he was hiding near the jar. When the snail lady came out of the jar, the young man grabbed her hands tightly and said, "Would you be my wife? You said you would share my meals." The lady blushed and then she nodded. The young man and the snail lady lived happily for many years as husband and wife.

My story

Scene 4

One day the king went hunting near the village where the happy couple lived. When he saw the snail lady, he was attracted by her beauty. "How come she's married to a farmer? I should make her my wife," said the greedy and unjust king. He called to the young man, "I challenge you to a contest. Tomorrow we'll see who can cut down trees faster. If you win, I'll give you half of my kingdom. But if you lose, you must give me your wife." When the young man heard this, his face turned white with worries. The snail lady fastened a note to her wedding ring, gave it to her husband and said, "Throw this ring into the ocean, and my father, the Dragon King will help you."

My story

212

Scene 5

The young man tossed the ring into the ocean. Amazingly the sea split apart and a path appeared, leading down into the sea. At the end of the road stood the Dragon King's Castle. The Dragon King welcomed him and gave him a gourd. The day of the contest arrived. The king ordered hundreds of soldiers to cut down the trees. When the young man opened the gourd, out came countless small men with small axes in their hands. They grew taller and taller instantly and cut down the trees in no time. After the trees were cut down they return to their orignal size and went back into the gourd.

My story

The king was angry. Instead of keeping his promise, he thought up another way to try and win the snail lady. "We have another contest tomorrow. This time we'll race our horses, and the first one to cross the river wins." said the mean king. The young man went to see the Dragon King and got a skinny horse. The king mounted his tall and strong horse and started off across the river just before the young man was ready. But the young man's horse ran as fast as lightening and won the contest.

My story

214

Scene 7

Of course the king did not keep his promise either. "This time we'll race boats," said the king, eager for another chance. The young man got a small rowboat from the Dragon King and floated his way out into the ocean. The king sailed out in his shiny, sparking new ship. The young man's little boat sped ahead of the bulky royal ship very fast. The king turned red and stamped his feet. But a big wave came up and swallowed him and his ship. He was nowhere to be found.

My story

Scene 8

Having beaten the king once and for all, the young man took the entire kingdom for himself. People were happy to have a new king and queen. The new king gave the poor food and riches that the former king had collected for himself. He loved his people and lived with his wife happily ever after.

My story